T0265958

Herbert Brooks Hatch, Jr. is one of America's living Fighter Pilot Aces from World War II. Hatch flew with the 71st Fighter Squadron, 1st Fighter Group, of the Army Air Force, out of Salsola, Italy. Except for a brief deployment to Corsica to cover the invasion of Southern France, he flew his fifty-nine missions out of Foggia #3. He holds the Distinguished Service Cross, the Distinguished Flying Cross and the Air Medal with 11 Oak Leaf Clusters. After the war, he spent his business career as an automobile dealer in Northern California, where he and his wife, Amy, raised their three children. Now retired, Hatch lives in LaConnor, Washington, where he enjoys reading and teaching "the art of golf." This is his first book.

an *Ace* and his Angel

Memoirs of a World War II Fighter Pilot

by Herbert "Stub" Hatch

Turner Publishing Company

Turner Publishing Company

Turner Publishing Company Staff
Editors: Bill Schiller & Lisa Thompson
Designer: Heather Warren

Copyright © 2000
Herbert B. Hatch, Jr.

Publishing Rights:
Turner Publishing Company

Library of Congress Catalog Card No:00-130176
Applied For
ISBN: 978-1-6816-2414-3

DEDICATION

This book is dedicated to the memory of the young men whom I knew and flew with in the United States Army Air Force in 1942-43-44-45. There were many but three occupy a special place in my heart:

Frank Helms
Killed, Santa Maria, CA, Feb 13, 1944

Chet Harvey
Killed, Santa Maria, CA, Feb 1944

Joe Jackson
Killed, Ploesti, Romania, June 1944

TABLE OF CONTENTS

ACKNOWLEDGEMETS

This little volume would never have seen the light of day without the support, encouragement, and efforts of two people. First is Amy, my dearly beloved wife of 61 years, who pushed, shoved, and browbeat me into writing these stories. She too lived those war years with me and her memories added much to mine. Second is my favorite brother-in-law, Charles F. Adams, who is a successful author himself and whose knowledge, enthusiasm, and belief in the value of my writing made the publishing of this book possible. I will be forever grateful for his efforts.

INTRODUCTION

I've said many times that there is no such thing as a hero—just some poor son-of-a-bitch who got his tail in a crack and fought like hell to get it out. Some were lucky and made it and some didn't. I was lucky—I made it.

This journey back to the war years seemed to take on its own life. It's kind of like digging around in an old attic—you keep finding things you had almost forgotten about. Remembering one instance recalls another one long since forgotten, which in turn brings up still another. It begins to become accumulative, and I'm constantly amazed at the clarity of these recollections from so long ago. I guess I'm like a lot of old goats. I can remember fifty years ago but can't remember what the hell I came into the kitchen for.

It has been fifty-three years since any of these experiences took place. I have done my best to reconstruct the events as they occurred and have attempted to make the conversations match the circumstances. I have tried not to embellish the incidents nor make the conversations more than what they probably were. What's on these pages is the best I could do looking back more than half a century.

PREFACE

Everyone who has lived long enough has, from time to time, asked "Why me - or why not me?" Those of us who have spent time in a war have had occasion to ask those questions more often than those who have not. The fickle finger of fate has spared many and killed many for reasons that are impossible to explain. It can be called "fate" or "luck," but the sheer inconsistency of life in a war is inexplicable. We who were spared can only remember those who were not and be thankful our number never came up.

I recall vividly three occasions when luck was on my side and let me live when the odds were not all that good.

The first occasion was in advanced training at gunnery school at Ajo, AZ, on a cold clear day. I was flying an AT6 on a gunnery flight and had climbed out to the target area to await my turn to shoot. It was very cold at even that altitude, and I had the cockpit heater on full blast and the canopy closed.

About fifteen minutes into the flight, I began to feel woozy and was having a little trouble breathing. I kept feeling worse and began to have trouble keeping the airplane straight and level and I developed a sudden painful headache. I knew something was terribly wrong and I decided to go back to base and land. For the moment, I wasn't just sure where I was, let alone where base was, but I turned and dived and tried to remember the landing procedures. I did remember that one of the first steps was to open the canopy so you could get out if something went wrong. So I slid the canopy wide open. There was, as always, a rush of cold, fresh air and, in a few minutes, I began to come to. I still felt terrible and had that splitting headache, so I continued back to land.

I got it down and, when I tried to climb out, I damn near fell out. I was taken to the infirmary and it wasn't long before I was back to normal except for the headache. The infirmary diagnosed the problem quickly and accurately—carbon monoxide poisoning. Later in the day, I learned the cockpit heater in that airplane was faulty and was pouring carbon monoxide into the cockpit. Another three or four minutes with the canopy closed and I would have been dead.

What prompted me to open the canopy? I wasn't in the landing pattern or anywhere near it, but I opened it anyway and stayed alive. Who knows why?

The second instance is a little more difficult to write about, because it concerns my father in his last two months with cancer. He had been diagnosed as having inoperable cancer of the liver and was given perhaps three to six months to live. This instance took place in January and he died Easter Sunday, April of 1944.

His greatest concern, as it had been all his life, was not for himself but for his family. This meant setting up his estate the best way he could. A large part of that estate was the value of the Chevrolet dealership we owned in Stockton, California. He arranged its sale in February, and since I was a minority shareholder in the corporation, my signature was required on the sale papers. I was midway through my RTU training at Santa Maria when all this occurred and Dad asked me to get leave and come to Stockton.

I went to my Squadron Commander, Capt. Mark Mourne, to request that leave. He was very sympathetic but reminded me that I was scheduled that weekend to go to March Field near L.A. to go through the altitude chamber tests. Those tests were to teach you the effects of anoxia, or oxygen deprivation, at high altitudes. Capt. Mourne suggested I trade my turn with somebody and free myself up the weekend.

Everything in the Army being based on the alphabet, I went looking for another "H." I got one of my squadron mates by the name of Hossick to swap. One week didn't seem to make much difference to him.

My wife, Amy, and I went to Stockton, went through the hours of legalese and the painful hours of trying to be cheerful and normal with Dad, knowing he was dying. It was the last time I ever saw him. That night on the news radio, we heard that an Air Force plane was missing and briefly wondered if it was one of ours.

We returned to the base at Santa Maria the next day and learned it was the March Field flight I was supposed to have been on. It had disappeared on the return flight. It wasn't found until June of '44. It had crashed on one of the Channel Islands many miles off course.

Once more, the finger of fate had not pointed at me, and I was still living while George Hossick was dead. Who knows why?

The third instance occurred on June 10th, 1944, on a mission to Ploesti, Romania. Reams have been written about that ill-fated day, but what has stayed in my memory is the fact that, out of the twelve of us involved in the actual fight, eight were shot down. My wingman's airplane was so badly damaged he barely made it back, and two were only partially engaged. Yet I came back with a fistful of victories and not one hole in my airplane. Those pilots who didn't come back were as good as I was, and some of them older hands at combat than I was. Yet I survived. Again I ask, why me? Or perhaps I should ask, why not me?

Somebody at the Ploesti debriefing made the remark, "Hatch, you had someone in the cockpit with you!" Maybe that "Someone" was my guardian angel.

1.) Fourteen Months As An Aviation Cadet

In 1942-43-44, pilot training in the Army Air Force consisted of four stages. The first was "Preflight" where you were taught to be a soldier and whipped into some kind of physical fitness. The second was "Primary Flight School" where you learned the rudiments of getting an airplane up and down. The third was "Basic Flight School" where you flew bigger airplanes, learned the basics of instrument flying and night flying. The fourth was "Advanced Flight School" with more powerful airplanes, basic formation flying, cross country flying, more night and instrument flying and transition into the airplane you would fly in combat. Each class going into Preflight was given a letter designating its position in that year. My original class was 43G.

Each stage was designed to be completed in approximately eight weeks, making the whole course about eight months, presuming you passed muster all along the line. The "wash-out" ratio was high, with the great majority of "washes" coming in Primary.

There was a time when I thought I'd be a Cadet for the duration. Here's why.

I went to Santa Ana for Preflight in late October of 1942. There were close to ten thousand cadets in all stages of the preflight training program. You became a serial number quickly. I still remember mine: 19092145. The physical training started the day you arrived. I was 24 years old, long removed from any athletics, and I found out fast that I was in

Not yet ready for war, "Stub" Hatch at Visalia Primary Flight School, October 1942.

lousy condition. The first two or three weeks damn near killed me. Above and beyond the calisthenics, running and close order drill, we were expected to spend our "spare time" in some type of athletic game. It was fall, so the game of "touch" football was in vogue.

There were a lot of ex-college types in the corps, some of whom had been football players in school. For them, the term "touch" football was used very loosely. My first career - delaying incident was the result of a game with one of those types on the other team. We were playing football with a softball since we didn't have a real football. On the play in question, I went out to receive a pass. The throw was a little high and I had to jump for it. While I was still in the air my opponent "touched" me and I fell forward, landing on my face and on my right hand which was wrapped around the ball. I'm sure I made a noise of some sort, because when I rolled over, I had dislocated and broken the little finger on that hand and had broken the third finger.

I wound up in the infirmary with nearly a full cast on my hand. We had just started taking what were called "motor tests" which were hand-eye coordination tests requiring considerable mobility of both hands. There was no way I could continue those tests, so down I went to squadron 3 which housed all the foul-ups, misfits and walking wounded. I stayed there while three classes passed me.

I finally talked a doctor into cutting the cast back to just two fingers and took the motor tests and passed even with that handicap and moved on with a new class.

One of the other games we played at Santa Ana was known as "speed ball." It was a cross between soccer and rugby and was nearly free from any rules. You could kick the ball, pick it up and run with it, or pass it - if you survived long enough. I played a game my last day at Preflight and took a solid kick in the groin (my cojones) which laid me low, but I sucked it up and left for Primary the next day.

We reported to Sequoia Field, went through the usual lower class hazing, and a day later went down to the flight line to be assigned instructors. I stood on the flight line as long as I could with my lower left groin hurting like hell. I finally had to fall out, tell the DI there was something wrong and report to the infirmary. I was advised that I had a ruptured hernia. That lump was my guts falling out. That afternoon I rode an ambulance to the Air Force Hospital at Hanford and was operated on the next day.

Things didn't look too bad. I was told I could expect to return to duty in three weeks at the most, which meant I'd only wash back one class. That didn't last long. A couple of days later I began feeling like hell, ran a fever and wound up really sick. After a flock of tests, I was told I had contracted "Valley Fever," medically known as coccidiomiosis, and that I wouldn't be released until it went away. It took four more weeks until I was cleared and given two weeks' sick leave to go home.

My wife, Amy, and my baby son, Brooks, were living with my parents in Stockton and I joined them there. We decided a little vacation was a great idea, so off we went to Carmel for a week's stay. The three of us had fun for a couple of days when suddenly I began to feel awful again. Amy took one look at me and ordered me into a hot bath tub. It didn't take long. I broke out all over in little red spots. My dearly beloved son, who had just recovered from a case of chicken-pox, had given it to me, and I was one sick Aviation Cadet.

Back we went to Stockton and called the doctor, who in turn, called Sequoia Field. I was told to stay home until I was completed cured. So I stayed another two weeks or so, and another class passed me. I was sure I'd never fly an airplane, let alone graduate from Cadets.

I finally got clearance to return and wound up in Class 43K. I had started out in "G." The only good thing that came out of all these troubles was that I been around for so long that I knew more than the other lower classmen, and I wound up in upper class as the Cadet Major in command of the entire Cadet Battalion.

The rest of my tour as a Cadet went according to the schedules—no more injuries and no more hospitals. I was Cadet Major at Primary and Cadet Captain Adjutant at Basic, as well as Cadet Squadron Commander at Advanced, all of which made my family very proud. They'd damn near given up hope.

2.) My Wife Saves My Career

My wife was an intricate part of, and lived every moment of my war career, either in fact or in thought. My P-38 was named "Mon Amy," a grammatically incorrect play on the French for "my friend." We had been married for over five years when I entered cadet training in 1943. Our son was born in 1940. Our relationship dated back to when we were fourteen and fifteen years old, respectively. Ironically, the day we met she hauled off and slapped my face with a full-arm swing, for using military-school profanity, which really got my attention. We went together, on and off, for five years until I finally convinced her I was worth keeping. We were married June 29, 1938, and even after 61 years, we're still together.

Near the end of my cadet training, I was stationed at Williams Field in Chandler, Arizona in Advanced Training. Amy and Brooks were living at the San Marcos Inn in Chandler, courtesy of my father. My $75.00 a month income might have paid for one or two days' room rent, but not the month or more they were there. I'm not sure of the dates, except that it had to be late November of 1943.

By then I had been checked out in the RP322's we flew, which were P-38's without the supercharger, and we were sent out on what was known as "familiarization flights" in which we were supposed to get accustomed to the airplane. On the day involved, I was up flying around, happy as a clam at high tide, when I saw a B-24 about 2000 feet below me and to my left. I immediately decided I should have a better look at this airplane since I probably would be escorting them at some time in the near future. I set up nicely for a high side pass and went screaming down. As I passed by the 24, I was pretty close - not dangerously, you understand - just enough to get their attention. I pulled up, did a half roll and wound up on the other side. The bomber pilot, true to type, shook his fist at me from his window, seemingly unimpressed with my flying. Then he pointed to me and to my rear. I was amazed to find another P-38, complete with a pilot who was wearing bright silver bars on his shoulders. He pulled up alongside me, looked me over carefully, and called me on the radio.

"What is your name?" he demanded.
"Cadet Hatch, Herbert B." I answered.
"What's your serial number?"
"19092145."
"Cadet Hatch - report to your Squadron Commander when you return to base."
"Yes sir," I gulped and banked away.

The rest of that flight was not very pleasant, and after I landed I reported as ordered. I don't remember what the Commander had to say, except for his final words: "Return to your quarters -you're grounded!"

I was one sick cadet. Graduation was in sight and I was looking at the very great possibility of washing out. I sat in my barracks for a long time and finally decided I'd better call Amy with the bad news. It goes without saying that she was as upset as I was, and our conversation wound up in tears. I went back to my room and sweated.

It seems that sometime earlier and quite coincidentally, Amy ran into Joanne, an old friend, while she and Brooks were in a Chandler drugstore. (Joanne's father owned the apartment we had lived in when we were first married.) After the "What are you doing here? etc." Amy explained that I was a cadet at Willy, and it turned out that Joanne's husband was a captain, also at Willy.

That night after my phone call, Amy needed someone to commiserate with, so she bundled up Brooks and went to see Joanne, the only person she knew in Chandler. She told her sad story to Joanne while Joanne's husband sat on the floor and played with Brooks. The Captain's name was Couch, and he was a returnee from the Pacific where he had flown 38's. After unburdening her soul, Amy went back to the hotel and, like me, tried to sleep.

The next morning I went to the flight line with my squadron and hid myself in the back of the ready room while the head instructor called out airplane numbers assigning cadets for the day's training flights. Everyone's name had been called except mine when he called out a number and said, "Hatch."

I jumped a foot and turned to my instructor and said, "I'm grounded!"

"Shut up and go get in the airplane," he growled. Nothing more was ever said about my "grounding," and I finally graduated with my class.

It wasn't until graduation day that Amy and I found out that Captain Couch was Director of Training at Williams Field. My good wife's tale of my troubles had moved the Captain's sympathy, and he had countermanded my grounding order. It was another case of my good luck - and certainly not the last time that having a wife turned out to be a lifesaver!

How a brand new 2nd Lieutenant feels when he comes home after graduation...Just Great!

3.) GETTING TO THE WAR WASN'T EASY

Most overseas assignments during WW2 were pretty straight-forward. You got your orders, climbed on a train or airplane, went to the point of debarkation, got on a ship or another airplane and went. When you arrived at the destination stated in your orders, you were met, assigned to an outfit, and began your war.

I was one of ninety-nine P-38 pilots sent to Hamilton Field to get orders to go overseas. None of us knew at that time what theater we were going to be sent to—South Pacific, England, Mediterranean or Aleutians. We were split up at Hamilton, given shots for every disease known to man, and received our orders. Thirty-three were sent to San Francisco to go to the South Pacific, sixty-five were put on a train for the East Coast, and one poor SOB was sent to the Aleutians. It was a cruel twist of fate for that pilot. He had been a G.I. in the Aleutians and had volunteered for flight training to get out of that miserable place only to be sent back. If I'd been him I might have gone over the hill.

Three days later, all of us got to Chicago in the A.M. where the train commander told us we could take off for twelve hours and then return for the ride to New York. We'd broken up into groups of two or three and I joined up with O.E. Johnson and Joe Jackson. The three of us had become good friends at Williams Field, and thanks to the Air Force's love for alphabetizing, we were in close contact throughout training and RTU. O.E. was from Portland while Joe was from Eugene, Oregon. I have no recollection of their families, if indeed we ever discussed them. Wartime friendships, even close ones, tended to be limited to the present, with little interest in the past and no conversation about the future beyond the next day.

So, we were in Chicago. O.E., Joe and I were hunting some whiskey. We found a kind-hearted vendor of booze who let us buy (for a highly inflated price) two fifths of Haig and Haig Pinch Bottle Scotch, which in those days was like finding gold. We were elated and left the store to find a taxi. Cold sober, I might add. In a little while, a cab came down the street. We hailed him and he pulled up near the curb. As I stepped off the curb to open the door of the cab I tripped, fell flat on my face, and down went the bottles of Scotch to the pavement. They shattered into a thousand pieces. I didn't cry, though I damned near did, and the words I uttered are not fit for print.

So, boozeless, we got back on the train and a couple of days later arrived in New York. We were transported to the Plaza Hotel on Park Avenue and told to do what we pleased. Our only duty was to call ATC every morning to see if we were on orders for that day. We were stuck, if that's the appropriate term, in New York for several days, how many I've forgotten. It was long enough to do a lot of sightseeing, see a couple of Broadway shows and generally have a ball until we went broke. In desperation, I went to the Waldorf-Astoria Hotel where I'd stayed with my parents years before, got hold of the concierge and sent a telegram to my father telling him I was broke and asking if could he wire me $400 at the Waldorf. I went back the next day and got the money, along with a telegram I'll never forget. It read, "Here is your money. Are you going to war or back to college? Dad"

Finally one morning I called ATC and was told to get my ass out to the airport immediately. Thirty-two others received the same message and we got on an Air Force bus and took off. We still didn't know where we were going, except that it had to be the European Theater. Not much time was wasted. Each of us was handed sealed orders with instructions, repeated again and again, not to open them until we were at least six hours out. I think the first guy to open his orders did so as soon as the gear was coming up on take-off.

We all took a look at our future real quick and discovered we were headed for El Aouina, Tunisia, wherever the hell that was. Some of the geography buffs got the word around that we were headed for North Africa, which was definitely in the Mediterranean Theater, and that there wasn't going to be any Merry Old England for this group.

We landed that night in miserable instrument weather at Stephansville, Newfoundland. We stayed that night and the next day, waiting for the weather to break. It was snowy, cold and foggy, so we just gathered around the stoves and waited. The next day it cleared enough and we took off. A couple of hours out, the crew let us know we were on our way to Casablanca, Morocco. We made a fuel stop at Tercera in the Azores and landed at Casablanca late that afternoon. There was a huge transient officers Quarters in tents on the field, and after we checked in, had something to eat, we wanted to see the "mysterious" city of Casablanca and have a look at North

Africa. A little questioning got us the recommendation to go to the Automobile Club, supposedly Casablanca's best night spot.

Our triumvirate of O.E., Joe and I found our way there, wide eyed at all the strange sights, smells and sounds. We settled down on the cushions that served as chairs, peered through the hanging strings of bead that divided the rooms, watched a belly dancer (pretty fat for us) and proceeded to get loaded on what was left of my four hundred dollars. When we decided it was time to return to the field, we discovered to our dismay that all the military transportation had called it a night and we were stuck several miles from the field in a strange city that was completely blacked out. After a while of stumbling around, we found a big black gendarme at the intersection of several streets. It quickly became apparent that the French he spoke had never been taught in my schools and that my fractured French was Greek to him.

I finally got him to understand we wanted to go to the airbase, but he just gave us a Gallic shrug indicating there was no transportation. At that moment, a local type came up to the intersection driving a sorry looking mule and a cart of sorts. The gendarme waved him down and after five minutes of conversation gave us to understand that for a price the local would take us to the field. I waved two or three American dollars at him and we climbed in. I don't know what he had been carrying in that cart, but the three of us stunk to high heaven when we got to the field.

The next morning, not too early, we made our way down to operations and asked how we were supposed to get to El Aouina. We were told to get our gear and get down to the flight line where there was a C47 headed that way in a little while. We looked all over for any of the rest of our group, found nobody, and decided we'd better go while the going was good. About 0900 we took off - just the three of us aboard with the crew and a bunch of cargo. It's a long way from Casablanca to El Aouina, and a C47 doesn't fly very fast, so it was late afternoon when we landed at our destination. The pilot landed, taxied over to a bunch of burned out hangars, and didn't even shut the engines down. The crew man opened the door, dropped the ladder out, and we climbed down. We turned around expecting him to throw our B4 bags off, only to see him pull up the ladder and shut the door. The pilot gave it the gun, taxied away and there we stood, yelling our heads off as we watched all our clothes fly away. All we had left was what was in our little "Dopp-Kit," a small case that held our toothbrushes, comb and brushes, a bar of soap and, in my case, an extra pair of undershorts and a pair of socks.

When we finally calmed down, we looked around at the airfield area. There wasn't much to see. There wasn't a soul in sight, but there was much evidence of war in the beat up hangars and wrecked airplanes. On the far side of the field there was a building in better shape than most, and it looked like it might have been a hotel, so we headed that way. When we got there we found a sign over a door that said "Hotel De Gink," and inside we found a G.I. sitting behind a makeshift counter. We showed him our orders and asked where we could find a P38 outfit. He looked at us as if we'd lost our minds and informed us that there hadn't been any Air Force people around Tunis for two or three months. He said that the war we were looking for was up in Italy. To say we were stunned is the understatement of the decade. It was evident that none of the rest of our group had made it this far, and we had no idea how we were going to get to Italy. It took some persuading, but we finally got him to give us a room for the night and an OK for one meal at the local mess hall. We didn't know it, but that was to be our last real meal for quite a while. It seems that each billeting establishment drew rations for the number of personnel assigned to that billet. No assignment meant no rations. That arrangement was going to keep us hungry for quite a while.

We knew that the war in North Africa was over, that Sicily had fallen and that Italy had been invaded. It's difficult at this late date to remember and put into words our feelings at that time. We were three young fighter pilots eager to get into a squadron and begin to use the hours and months of training we'd gone through. We'd left the states fully expecting our orders to take us to a place where that eagerness could be used. Instead we had wound up a continent away from the war, unmet, unwanted and, to all intents and purposes, totally lost. We had no orders that legally could take us beyond where we were because we belonged to no organization. We felt lost, frustrated and, yes, scared. We knew we had to do something, but we didn't know what or how. We were pretty low that night, but by the next morning we felt a little better and decided we'd just have to figure out some way to get to our war. It's a good thing we couldn't reach the idiot who cut the orders sending us to El Aouina. We'd have killed the bastard.

We waited two days. During that time, we found a veritable graveyard of wrecked enemy aircraft—109s, JU88s, JU52s and some others. We'd never seen anything except pictures of Jerry aircraft, so we crawled around, under and over the whole mess, getting our first contact with the real thing. When we came out of the other end of the wrecking yard, we only walked about ten yards when we heard somebody yell "Halt!" We halted and met a G.I. sentry, fully armed and unhappy.

"Where the hell did you come from?" he asked.

"We just walked over from the Hotel De Gink," I answered, "and wanted to take a look at these enemy aircraft."

The sentry looked at us with his mouth open. "You came clear across the boneyard," he gasped.

"Yep," I said.

"Jesus Christ," he gulped, "I don't know why you're still alive. That place is booby-trapped all over to keep the WOGS from stealing!" We stared at him, stared at each other and went back to the hotel - the long way around. Apparently, my angel looked after me when I was on the ground too.

We spent all the rest of the time trying to find a way to get to Italy and scrounging something to eat. We finally found a Major in Tunis who would listen to our tale of woe. He gave us a cup of coffee and a sandwich and arranged to get us on a British C47 that was going to Naples the next morning.

We boarded the plane, sans breakfast, the only Americans among a full load of Limey soldiers, including a British Brigadier General who promptly got airsick and caused the poor orderly all kinds of problems. Everybody tried to look the other way. The poor guy was terribly embarrassed.

We landed at Naples, found the ops office and asked where the 38s were. After considerable conversation, somebody said he thought the 15th Air Force was over near Foggia, which didn't mean much to us. The gang in ops went to bat for us, and in about a half hour we were on another C47 headed for Foggia.

We walked into the ops office on the Foggia airport and started asking questions again and by now we'd gotten close enough to the action to get some answers. The 15th's fighter wing headquarters was at a place called Torremaggiore. "Good," we said, "how do we get there?"

One of the sergeants in the office said he'd call them and tell them there were some pilots down here. We were amazed. Here was someone who not only could, but would, help us. The ops guy got the call through and we were advised to stay put and there would be transportation in an hour or so. We looked at each other and smiled. We'd made it! We even managed to badger the local mess sergeant into giving us a sandwich and a cup of coffee. I have to digress for a moment here to set the stage for the rest of the story. We'd been in the same uniforms, Woolen Class A complete with blouse, for the better part of three weeks. North Africa and southern Italy in the spring are not places for wool uniforms in the first place, and such a uniform, worn steadily for the period of time we'd worn ours, did nothing for our appearance, not to mention our smell. We were dirty, wrinkled, and generally pretty miserable looking.

In an hour or so, what should show up but a 6 by 6 truck with an open bed, no cover tarp and benches along the sides. That was our transportation. We climbed aboard and off we went in a cloud of dust that lasted all the way to Torremaggiore. I think all the roads in Italy are dusty.

As bad as we looked before that hour's ride, that 6 by 6 finished us off. We were really a sad looking bunch.

When we reached Torremagiore, we pulled up in front of a magnificent Italian villa complete with wrought iron gates, brick fences and lush green lawns. We piled out wide-eyed, and the driver said, "G2 is upstairs in the building on the left."

We went in, climbed the stairs, found the sign that said G2 and walked in proud of ourselves and expecting a warm greeting for having found our way to the war. What we got was a non-flying Major who took one look at us, studied our orders and chewed our asses out for looking like bums and for taking so long to report in. When he got through discussing our shortcomings, he ordered us to go back outside and wait while he decided what to do with us.

Second Lieutenants don't argue much with Majors, but those were three damned mad Lieutenants who went and stood in the courtyard of that villa. It wasn't the reception we had expected, and we were so damned mad, tired and hungry we didn't even talk to each other.

We stood, leaning on the fence for about ten minutes, when in through the gate came a staff car with a little flag on the fender bearing a single star. The car pulled up right in front of us, the driver jumped out, opened the door and a Brigadier General got out. As fed up as we were, we decided that protocol required us to salute a general, so we got almost to attention and saluted.

The General started to return the salute, took a good hard look at us, stopped, walked over and said, "You're the sorriest looking bunch of officers I've ever seen. Who are you and what's your excuse for your appearance?"

I flipped my lid. I was so damned mad, tired and hungry, I didn't care if I got court-martialed that evening, and I took off. I spent the next ten minutes telling the General where we'd been, what our orders had said, how we got there. I also told him that I, for one, was damned tired of getting chewed out. I thought O.E. and Joe would faint. Lieutenants didn't talk to Generals like that, and they were sure we'd be shot at sunrise. When I finished - somewhat cooled off - so did I.

To our amazement, the General - whom we found out later was BG Crothers in command of the 15th Air Force Fighter Wing - made no attempt to shut me up. He listened to all my outbursts, including what I thought of his G2 Major, until I finally ran down. He took another look at us, turned to his driver and said, "Get that Major down there." In about twenty seconds, the Major raced up and got the chewing out of his career for the way he had treated us. It seemed the General agreed with me as to our reception. We listened and did our best to keep a straight face while the General had his say. When he finished, he dismissed the Major, turned to his driver and said, "Take these men to my quarters. See to it they get a shower, and find some clean uniforms for them." Then he turned to us and said, "You'll have dinner with me this evening and I'll assign you tomorrow!"

That General will always be our favorite General. As far as we were concerned, he deserved four stars.

That's about the end of this story. We got cleaned up, and during dinner we filled in some of the blanks my tirade had left. When we told him there were thirty other pilots somewhere between Casablanca and Italy, he flipped his lid. The 15th had been hurting for replacement pilots for a long time. I'll never know how he did it, but those thirty pilots were in squadrons within three days. He even got our B4 bags back. We all went to the 71st at our request, and I only saw him once more. That was the day Major General Twining pinned the DSC on me. Crothers came over and congratulated me.

Well, that's how I got to the war. From Santa Maria to Torremaggiore took more than three weeks, which wasn't quite as long as it took me to get home after my tour of duty. But that's another story.

Major General Twining confers the Distinguished Service Cross on 1st Lieutenant Hatch. June 1943

4.) Buying Vegetables Can Be Dangerous

One of the many things which made life less than ideal in Italy in 1944 was the lack of fresh fruits and vegetables in our diet. It wasn't the fault of the cooks, but simply the fact that there were none in the regular G.I. issue. One can get tired of canned and dried foods very quickly, and try as the poor cooks might, they couldn't make the stuff they were sent taste like home. We had heard rumors that there was a farmers' market down in Bari where such goodies could be purchased very reasonably, but no one had checked it out.

It was in late June or early July when there was a standdown for the whole Air Force (i.e. no mission). For lack of anything better to do, O.E., Joe and I decided to find out if the rumors were true. We got a jeep from the squadron motor pool and headed south. It was nearly 75 miles from our base to Bari on a not-so-hot road, but with little traffic we made it in about two and half hours. We found the market down near the waterfront and the rumors were correct. There was a lot of produce of every kind. I saw my first Italian tomatoes. The darn things were square, not round, and the watermelons were round as a basketball and a funny color, but they were *fresh!* And the prices, as I remember, were really cheap. I recall that the watermelons were three cents a pound in invasion currency!

We loaded up and started back to the base. We hadn't gone more than a third of the way when we encountered a whole Brigade of Free French armored vehicles. That brought the fast lane to a screeching halt, and we spent a slow and dusty hour trying to pass tanks and armored vehicles on a road that didn't lend itself to passing anything.

We had almost reached the head of the column when O.E. hollered, "Look at that damn fool airplane!" I was driving and, just as I heard him holler, that airplane started shooting. It wasn't more than a hundred feet off the ground—going like hell—and spraying the landscape with cannon and machine-gun fire. "That's a 109," I yelled and slammed on the brakes. The

O.E. Johnson gets drinking water from the "Lister Bag," the only source of drinking water at the airfield.

road at that point ran through an olive orchard with a ditch on both sides and stone walls between the ditch and the orchard. The first 109 went screaming past us, followed by a second one banging merrily away. I don't really remember bailing out of the jeep, but I was joined in the ditch by my passengers, one of whom lit on top of me, with no apology. As you can imagine, there was confusion and chaos among the French as well as us. There hadn't been any enemy over Italy in many months and where those two Jerries came from God only knows, but they were having a field day. They made their pass north to south, then made a 180 and did it again south to north. By then some of the French got some guns working and bravely, if ineffectually, started firing back.

The whole shebang didn't take more than six or eight minutes, but from where I was laying, I was damned sure those 109s had me and me alone in their sights. I have flown some strafing missions, and know damned well that individual targets are almost impossible to pick out when you're clocking a couple of hundred miles an hour at fifty feet. But at the time I wasn't at all convinced they weren't after me.

Those 109s made three passes over the convoy and headed east as fast as they could. They had caused considerable damage to the French, and it took a while to get things unscrambled. The dive in the ditch didn't help

Fighter escorts (aka little friends) pulling contrails over a B-17 formation.

our looks much, ditches being what they were in Italy, but our jeep wasn't hit and our tomatoes, watermelons and other stuff was intact, so we saddled up and headed home. It took a lot of convincing of our squadron mates to make them believe our story. They were a hellova lot more interested in what we had brought home than they were in any of our troubles.

The *Stars and Stripes* newspaper carried a little story of the raid later on, which confirmed our veracity but generated little sympathy. I couldn't help but think those two 109 pilots had a lot of guts to fly across the Adriatic, look for a target, and shoot the place up right in the middle of the whole 15th Air Force. There were real fighter pilots on both sides of that war.

5.) FUN AND GAMES WITH THE LOCALS

There were many days in my tour of duty in Italy, as there were in everybody's, when we did not fly missions. Most of those days were sheer boredom. There were no recreational facilities in camp and damned little sightseeing in the vicinity, except for a couple of ruined castles. Our only "R&R" was the Red Cross club in Foggia which dispensed coffee and doughnuts and had the added attraction of American girls. They were all off limits away from the club. I discovered that one of them was a girl I had dated when I was in military school in Boonville, Missouri, back in the early 1930s. Her name was Ann Busiek, and we had old home week for a while

Hatch gets ready to take to the air. Foggia flight line, 1944.

and later I took her sailing out of Manfredonia. She had married a boy from Kemper-Busiek, who became a 51 pilot and was shot down over France. That's when she joined the Red Cross.

Often on non-mission days we had occasion to make engineering flights to check repairs that had been made to various airplanes. Those flights generally became chances to have some fun. The Italians did not love the 38s very much. Prior to the invasion of Italy, the 38 groups from Africa were sent to the Foggia area to strafe the German airfields. The raid was an enormous success, destroying more than half the Luftwaffe based there. In the process, one hellova lot of the Italian population got shot up. Understandably, this caused some disaffection among the locals. We were well aware of the their dislike of us and made it a practice to update their sentiment whenever possible.

As an example, I remember a day I was testing an airplane, and that included seeing how low the airplane would fly. I found a narrow road that ran from the Foggia plains up toward the mountains to the west and into a small village. I won't say I was kicking up dust from the road, but when I got to the village I was well below the rooftops, headed right up the main drag. This was great fun until I discovered my wingspan was greater than the width of the street! It was too late to pull up and too late to turn. I was indicating about 220 and was in deep trouble. I did the only thing I could. I flipped the airplane on its side and went through town with the wings in vertical position. I can still remember a split second sighting of a fat Italian lady standing on a little wrought iron balcony, looking down at me as I went by. She was even more surprised than I was. I didn't go back there again. The streets were just too narrow.

Another time I was out buzzing the area when I saw an old Italian slowly making his way along another of those dusty roads in his one horse wagon. They used a one axle wooden wagon with big wooden wheels, drawn by one horse. This guy had evidently been out gathering what wood there was and was headed home. I couldn't resist. I laid the airplane on the deck, coming up behind him. You couldn't hear a 38 approaching - it was almost noiseless from in front. When I went over him at about five feet, his whole world came apart! I looked in the rear view mirror and roared. The horse went one way, the wagon went another, and the poor driver went flying, with his load of sticks going all over the countryside. Later I thought about it and was ashamed of myself. I could have hurt the horse.

We had a pilot in the squadron named Spitler, who could fly lower longer than any pilot I ever knew. He had a couple of little habits that none of the rest of us had any desire to copy. His idea of fun was to take his plane out on the Adriatic, trim it nose up and stick that part of a 38's rudder that hung below the booms in the water and make twin wakes. Now that's flying low! When he got tired of that, he'd go looking for some of the fishing boats that worked out of the little port near us and see if he could buzz them low enough that his prop wash would hit their sails and tip them over. He didn't make many friends among the fishermen.

There were a few other pilots who had favorite ways to aggravate the locals, but after a while the resident AMG, American Military Government, caught so much flack from the Italians that we had to quit. They threatened to court-martial the next guy they caught.

Looking back, I have to admit that we weren't very nice guys. After all, Italy had quit the war and joined our side - after we'd licked them - and maybe we should have been more thoughtful. But it sure was fun while it lasted.

6.) A Once-In-A-Lifetime Sight Over Munich

One day in the spring of 1944, the Air Force Command decided to show the Germans what air power really was. They picked the city of Munich for the demonstration.

As a target, Munich was about as far south as the 8th Air Force could get, and about as far north as the 15th Air Force, and particularly the fighters, could fly and return. It meant a long trip over enemy territory all the way. The plan called for the 8th to reach Munich about 1000 and bomb steadily, wing after wing, until 1230. At 1300 hours, the 15th was to arrive and bomb until 1530. That is a full five hours of continuous bombing and required a maximum effort by both Air Forces.

The day chosen just happened to be one of those rare days we sometimes got over the continent of Europe. There wasn't a cloud in the sky and for once we had unlimited visibility.

The 1st Fighter Group drew the job of target cover for the first wing of heavies from the 15th. We were just a tad early at the I.P. and had to make a 360 over the target as the bombers arrived. We circled at 26,000 and watched. The target was already completely covered by smoke and dust and the flak was comparatively light. There was no enemy fighter activity.

The sight I could see over the target was one which I never expect to be seen again and one which kept us all silent. As far as I could see to the northwest, and I could see many miles, there was a solid line of 8th Air Force bombers going home and as far as I could see to the south, there was a solid line of 15th heavies coming to the target. Everywhere I looked, there were 8th and 15th fighter squadrons and groups going and coming. I couldn't even guess, with any accuracy, how many of our airplanes I could see, but counting all the bombers and fighters there had to be more than a thousand. The 15th alone put up 800 bombers that day and the 8th was a bigger Air Force.

It was the greatest armada of air power ever seen or will ever be seen again. I can still remember the feeling of absolute invincibility it gave me and the conviction that the war was won.

I don't know of any other mission on which both strategic Air Forces went to the same target at the same time. Being a part of that one was a special privilege.

I've often wondered what it must have been like in Munich that day. Five solid hours of 500 pound bombs falling without a let-up boggles the imagination.

7.) A Wingman Comes Back From The Dead

During the summer of 1944, almost all our missions were high altitude missions escorting the heavies of the 15th Air Force. We had a few strafing missions and one forgettable dive bombing mission, but most of the time we were high above the ground. With the 51s pulling fighter sweeps ahead of the bombing force, we went many times without any contact with enemy forces at all. It got to be pretty dull after a while and a little excitement would have been welcome.

It was on the way home from one of those "milk runs" that I got myself and my whole squadron in a mess of trouble. I was leading the 71st that day, not for the first time, and as usual we let down from oxygen level so those of us who smoked could take off our masks and light up. We were cruising along somewhere over Yugoslavia when one of our group called and said, "Red Leader - look at the little train down there at about ten o'clock." I looked and there it was — a little train of about four cars and an engine, running along a fairly wide valley between two mountain ridges. It was just good too resist, and the urge for a little action took over.

I hit the radio button and said, "O.K., Cragmore, drop belly ranks and follow me down in trail." We peeled off and headed down. I chose to make the pass from west to east because there was more room between the hills and the track on the west side of the valley. Art Hoodechek was a relatively new boy, and he was flying my wing as number two.

Everything looked lovely as I leveled off to make my run - and then all hell broke loose. The sides of those four cars dropped off and exposed multiple mount 40mm Bofors, two to a car, and the flak started flying. I hit the radio and yelled, "Break it off, Cragmore, break it off." It was too late for me to stop my pass, so I opened fire, blew the engine up, and tried to spray the Bofors. But it was too late for Hoody. They nailed him dead center, and I watched him in my rear view mirror pull straight up about a thousand or twelve hundred feet, stall out, roll over and crash. I saw no chute, nor did any of the others, and I was one sick squadron leader. I had heard of those Q trains, as they were called, but had never seen one before. Not only had I lost a pilot and plane, but I had disobeyed an order. We had been expressly forbidden to go strafing when we were on escort missions. I was not looking forward to explaining Hoody's loss when I got back to the field.

I caught hell, which I deserved, but also got a C+ from the intelligence officer for the information on the Q train, because it justified their previous warnings. This had been the first actual sighting.

Eventually, of course, I finished my tour and returned to the States, and my wife and my son. It was the practice in those days to give returning pilots a couple of weeks at home and then have them report to a Rest and Rehabilitation Center for some physical and mental evaluation. For those of us on the West Coast, the Center was the Del Mar Club in Santa Monica, one of the plush resorts prior to the war. Wives were welcome, and Amy went with me.

We had been there four or five days and were sitting in the dining room having lunch when a ghost entered the dining room. Amy says I turned white as a sheet, jumped up and yelled clear across the room, "Hoody!" Surely enough it was Hoodechek, alive and in perfect health. We had old home week for about an hour and what follows is his story.

When he got hit, his airplane caught fire immediately and his only chance was to try to bail out. He pulled straight up as I had seen and when the plane started to stall he popped the canopy and went over the side. He said his chute opened, and he and the plane hit the ground almost together. He hit pretty hard but didn't break anything, and his first reaction was to get the hell out of the area as fast as he could. He started running east toward the nearest hills. There was no pursuit and he just kept going. You do funny things under circumstances like that. After a few minutes of running he became aware he still had his bright orange Mae West on and decided he had to get rid of it fast. Since he was running through a field of pumpkins, he tore the vest off, wrapped it around a pumpkin and took off again.

He kept going east and up into the mountains and forests without seeing a soul until late that afternoon. He came around a bend in the trail he had been following and ran into what he said was the meanest looking s.o.b. he'd ever seen, complete with a submachine gun and a nasty look. Hoody said he stopped in his tracks, raised his hands over his head and froze. He spoke to this character and used the phrase we had been taught to use "Americanski Piloto." Nothing happened. The guy didn't speak or move - just kept that gun pointed at Hoody's belly. He tried again with the same result. Then he had a bright idea; he showed the guy his wings and this guy let go a burst from his machine gun, right into the ground at Hoody's feet. Hoody said it took a little while for him to come down out of a tree, but the gunner made him slowly undo his flight suit and took the 45 that Hoody had forgotten he was wearing. Still with no words, he was waved up the trail and he set out with this mean looking guy behind him.

To make a long story a little shorter, Hoody had been picked up by one of Titos Partisans and that night was taken to a camp where he found several other American air crew members who had been shot down and rescued by the Partisans. The group spent some time in that camp and one night was taken down to a field where a C47 came in, loaded them all up, and took them back to Italy.

I've seen Hoody several times at the 1st Fighter Group reunions. He never seemed to hold it against me for getting him shot down, and I can tell you he was a welcome surprise in that dining room.

8.) ONE OF LIFE'S LITTLE MYSTERIES

One of my most unusual experiences, if not the most unusual, took place early in June of 1944. The squadron had been assigned to escort some heavies into Romania, to a target I've forgotten, and I was put on the mission. It was during the time my crew chief and I were going nuts trying to figure out why I was losing the supercharger on my right engine time after time. I suffered something like eight or nine aborts, one right after another, and this mission was one of those aborts. When we reached the altitude, the turbos were supposed to kick in my right engine but they pooped out and I was forced to turn back. It was early enough in the trip that the spares hadn't gone home yet, so one filled in for me. I dropped down to an altitude where I didn't need the extra boost and started home.

You're always a little nervous all by yourself in enemy territory, and when I spotted a B24 lumbering along below me, I immediately dropped down and formed up on him, figuring he wouldn't mind an escort. I checked his call sign on my mission notes and switched to his channel and called him. I got no response. I tried again and got no response. I could see the pilots in the cockpit, and the top gunner, but I got no happy wave or any sign that they knew I was around.

I became aware that the 24 was slowly but steadily losing altitude, even though all four engines seemed to be running. At least all four props were turning, though there was no way I could tell if they were putting out full power. I was getting more curious by the minute and decided to stick around and see what happened. We went along for quite some time on the same heading and had gotten out over Yugoslavia and were down to about five or six thousand when the 24 abruptly turned 90 degrees left. I tagged along wondering what the hell he was doing, when suddenly the crew started bailing out one after another. I slowed down even more and watched chute after chute pop until I had counted ten in the air. The last guy out had a problem. His chute split a panel when it opened and he was falling faster than the others. Since the 24 and I were still flying south, I didn't see the crew hit the ground but I figured they must have landed pretty close together.

All this was taking place over an area that for a change wasn't full of mountains. Their 24 was slowly turning to the left, losing altitude, and to me it appeared it was going to come down just to the south of a small lake in an area that was flat and looked muddy. I flew down under the 24. The bomb bay doors were open, there were no bombs in the bay and there were no people left aboard. I pulled up above the 24 and tried to decide what to do. It seemed to me that, if the 24 bellied in where it looked like it was headed, then it wasn't going to suffer a lot of damage and would afford a fine chance for the enemy to have a B24 to play with - not to mention a Norden bomb sight which was supposed to be very secret. So, I thought, why not shoot the damned thing down and destroy it and keep it out of enemy hands? The decision didn't take long. I dropped back about a hundred yards, armed my guns and started shooting.

I aimed at the left wing engines where I thought the gas tanks were. There was no question about getting hits because it was a sitting duck, but the damned thing wouldn't burn. I'd seen bombers hit with short bursts of fire from 109's and 190's and go down on fire, but I shot up almost all of my ammunition - four 50's and a 20mm cannon - before the left outboard engine caught fire and fell off and the plane rolled over and went in. To this day I haven't figured out why it took so many hits to get it to go down.

When I saw it finally hit the ground, I woke up to the fact that I was still some distance from home and close to being out of ammo. I decided that I'd better get my ass home. I got back to Foggia 3 with no trouble, and when I landed I had my crew chief pull the gun camera cartridge and give it me. He and I left the engine problem for later, and I headed to operations to tell my story, all full of curiosity and concern as to what the reaction of the brass was going to be.

The operations officer and the intelligence officer listened to my story, took the gun camera film and said they'd check the whole thing out. That was the last I ever heard of it. For days I asked if there was any information, asked if I could see the film, and each time got nothing. About a month later, our group commander and I ran into each other at Group Headquarters and he made the remark that I should be complimented on my actions.

That was, and is, the sum and substance of the whole affair. I still can't figure out why the crew of that bomber chose to bail out. The airplane was flying, they were not more than an hour from their base at most, and pretty much free of the possibility of any enemy action. All I can guess is that they either felt the airplane wouldn't make it across the Adriatic or they were tired of the war and decided to get the whole thing over for good.

A strange but true story and one that I still wonder about.

9.) WE TEACH A BOMB GROUP NOT TO BE SMART-ASSES

As I've said before, our only source of entertainment in Italy was a trip to the Red Cross Club in Foggia for coffee and doughnuts. (And a chance to ogle the Red Cross Girls.)

As you came into the small building which housed the Club, on the wall, there was a space for messages with both a blackboard and a bulletin board on which you could pin written messages. It afforded about the only means of communication between groups and individuals in the theater.

One day in late June or early July, O.E. and I and another 71st pilot took the trip to Foggia. There was a stand-down for the whole airforce that day and the club was fairly crowded. As we walked in, we saw a large block lettered message pinned to the bulletin board that stopped us in our tracks. In read, "Will the P38s that buzz our field please get off of oxygen," signed Bomb Group XXX.

We looked at the message, looked at each other, and without a word yanked the paper from the board and headed back out the door followed by some rude noises from somewhere in the room. We piled into our jeep and took off for our field, barged into our C.O.'s office and dropped the paper on his desk.

"Major," I said, "I don't think we should let an insult like this go unanswered. Don't you agree?"

He read and re-read the message and got a grim look on his face. "I certainly do agree, Lieutenant. There will be a practice mission for the squadron at 1400 hours!"

At 1400 hours, sixteen of us took off with Bob Spitler leading, which pleased us no end. As I've said before, Spit could fly lower longer than any pilot I ever knew.

We formed up, climbed to about 4000 feet, and headed for that bomb group's field. We circled twice to make sure there was no one in the pattern and Spit came on the horn. "We'll make one pass in formation right down the runway. After that it's every man for himself. For God's sake don't run into each other!"

We went south far enough to be pretty much out of sight of the field, and then Spit laid it on the deck and in we went. I've forgotten what position I was flying in, but I was on the left edge of the runway close to some parked airplanes. That first pass sure got everyone's attention. Sixteen P38s can make a helluva lot of noise and everyone on that field was out of doors in nothing flat to see what was going on and that was just the start. We broke up our formation as we pulled up from the pass and took off on our own. We must have beaten that place up for fifteen minutes. There were 38s coming from every direction at altitudes best described as low, lower and lowest. How we made it with no mid-airs I'll never know.

I have one vivid recollection of my part in the action. I saw a G.I., evidently an armorer, start to walk across an open space with a 50 caliber on his shoulder. He was the hard-nosed type who was going to get his job done regardless of all these idiots flying around. I turned towards him about 200 yards out and laid it on the grass. He was looking directly at me and wasn't about to let me worry him. It look about three seconds to change his mind. I wasn't any higher off the ground than his head level and discretion suddenly took preference over valor. He dropped the gun and fell flat on his face just as I screamed over him. I looked in my rear view mirror and he'd rolled over onto his back and was shaking both fists at me. I think if that gun had been fireable he'd have used it. I didn't blame him!

We finally formed up again and crossed their field at a reasonable height, rocked our wings and went home. I heard later that there was some flak from the bomb group's C.O., but, when told of the earlier message, he quieted down.

We never saw another sarcastic message at the Red Cross Club.

10.) Losing Your Temper Can Kill You

One of the few bad characteristics of the P38 models prior to the "L" was the tendency to get going too fast in a dive. They were heavy airplanes for their time and had a very small frontal surface. Those two features combined to make acceleration in a nearly vertical dive extremely fast, particularly at high altitudes. When the P-38 "L" model was finally delivered to us in late summer '44, it was a totally different airplance. It had hydraulic boost on the ailerons and most important, dive flaps which ended the fear of over-speed in the dive.

We did not know much about Mach speed, in fact I never heard the word until after the war. But we knew we could hit what was then called "compressibility," which later translated into the sound barrier. When a 38 hit compressibility, the airflow over the controls was disturbed and became so strong that it effectively locked the controls and they could not be moved. If the dive continued, the airplane would "tuck under," going past vertical into a partially upside down position. Once that configuration occurred, there was no return. Any recovery from compressibility at altitude depended on trying to slow the airplane down and hoping the denser air at a lower altitude would permit recovery. I found out about this problem the hard way; I let myself get carried away.

One day in July, the lst was assigned as target cover for a group of 24s who were to bomb Linz, Germany. The mission started out routinely. We picked up the bombers at their I.P. and followed them in. We stayed our usual 2000 to 3000 feet above them, looking for enemy aircraft level or above us where they usually came from. Linz is on the Danube in a canyon with high mountains on the north and south sides, making the bomb run predictably east to west.

Suddenly somebody called, "Cragmore, there's bandits coming up through the flak from below." We were amazed. We'd never seen Jerry attack through their own flak nor from below the bombers. Red Leader called, "Drop belly tank and let's go!" We were at about 25,000 feet, the bombers at about 23,000.

As we started down, we saw something else brand new to us. The Jerrys were firing air to air rockets, the first we'd ever seen. They succeeded in hitting several bombers and parachutes began to appear as crews bailed out. We tore into the Jerry fighters and our formation broke up as each of us went after individual targets. I took after two 190s to my right and below. One split-essed back under me and the other dove toward two or three chutes and started shooting at them. The sight of that damned German trying to kill those defenseless parachuters made me blow my top! I jammed all the power on and went almost straight down after him. He broke off and dove away and I started shooting. It was far too long a range to be effective, but I was so mad I didn't care. I evidently hit the radio button as well as the gun trigger, because later back at the field the gang kidded me, saying all they could hear on the radio was me cussing and my guns firing.

The 190 turned left, and when I tried to follow I couldn't move my controls. I don't remember what my indicated airspeed was, but it must have been in excess of 450-500 MPH and I was going almost straight down. I realized that I'd hit that barrier I'd been told about and that I'd better quit worrying about that Jerry and start worrying about Hatch.

There was no thought of bailing out. Even if I could have gotten out, the speed would have killed me. I had to stay with the airplane and try to slow it down. I chopped all power off, shoved the prop controls into full high pitch, and reached for the elevator trim tab. I began to slowly crank nose up trim and discovered I could hold my breath and pray at the same time. I have no recollection of the duration of the dive and a very short recollection of the plane pulling out of it because, when it did, it went all at once. God knows how many Gs I pulled. I blacked out, my oxygen mask pulled off, and I was out like a light.

When I came to, the airplane was going almost straight up and on the edge of a stall. My nose was bleeding, my mouth was full of blood and I was barely conscious. I was awake enough to feel the stall

At Santa Maria, Hatch inspects the first real P38 to fly.

and had sense enough to push the nose down and add power. It damned near stalled again because of the elevator trim.

It took several minutes to get me and the airplane trimmed up and to begin to think straight. I looked around but couldn't see another airplane, I decided I'd had enough for one day and headed home. I obviously got there O.K.

How that 38 stayed together I'll never know. I had to have pulled more than nine Gs, and yet there was little or no damage to the airplane. The empennage had to be re-trimmed, but that was about it. Another testimonial to the P38. And another case of a thoroughly chastened fighter pilot who never again dove after an enemy aircraft.

11.) REMEMBERING THE "TUSKEGEE ANGELS"

It has only been in the last few years that the 332nd Fighter Group has begun to get the recognition that it has so long deserved. The 332nd was attached to the 15th Air Force in 1944 and flew many missions out of Italy. They were the only wholly black unit in the Air Force, totally segregated from the time they entered training at Tuskegee, Alabama, until the war's end. It may be hard to understand in this age, but in the 1940's the United States "apartheid" was nearly as strict as that of South Africa. The "coloreds," or the negroes, were separated from the whites in almost every walk of life.

In 1942 somebody thought they should take a gamble and see if blacks could be taught to fly. The training was really severe. I don't know what the wash rate was, but it was horrendous. I'd bet that half the white boys who went through our Cadet training wouldn't have made it at Tuskegee. There were about four squadrons finally formed and three of them became the 332nd Fighter Group. Originally, they were equipped with P-40s, and with that airplane there was no way they could compete with the Luftwaffe. In the early summer of 1944, the group was sent back to North Africa and re-equipped with P51Ds, took a month's training in that airplane, and rejoined the 15th. Inside of a few weeks they became the hottest Group in the Air Force.

They were still segregated as far as any off-base activities were concerned, and the rest of us never saw them on the ground. In the air, their 51s with the bright red tail and spinner were recognized and respected. My personal contact with them occurred on a day in August and has always tickled me.

On this particular mission, I was leading the 1st Group on escort to the Vienna area. We were scheduled to be target cover for a wing of 24s, and we were supposed to be relieved by another Group which would be withdrawal cover. We made our rendezvous, covered the bombers for the I.P., the withdrawal point, but no relief showed up. We were getting low on fuel and I started getting complaints from some of the pilots. I was looking all over for some help and finally spotted a gaggle of 51s. When they got a little closer, I could see their red tails and knew they were the 332nd. I scrounged around in my mission info trying to find their call sign for the day and finally found them listed as "Betty." We were "Sandsail" for that day. I switched to the right frequency and called.

"Betty One, this is Sandsail One, do you read?"

Back came the response. "Betty here — read you loud and clear."

"Betty One, we're supposed to get relief and it hasn't showed up. I've got some planes getting low on fuel. Could you take these bombers over so we can go home?"

Back came the reply in the deepest bass voice I ever heard, with a real southern accent, "Sandsail One, we gonna be around fo' a while, you g'wan home." I couldn't help laughing. The voice — the phraseology - the accent - was almost a caricature, but one that gave me a great feeling. I thanked him and headed back to base. We all made it with no sweat and had a good laugh about the whole affair when we got there.

In retrospect, I guess we were as guilty of racial bigotry as everyone else. We also were products of the times. But be that as it may, I've never forgotten that voice. There are times when I can still hear that Group leader as plain as I did that day.

12.) A Novel Kind Of Flak

The invasion of Southern France was made in early August of 1944. For several weeks before the invasion, the 15th Air Force ran missions from Italy to France in order to "soften up" the defenses. One of those missions was flown by the 1st Fighter Group in late July as a low level strafing mission near Toulon.

The 71st was the lead squadron for that mission, led by Bob Spitler. Spit, as he was familiarly known, loved to fly low, as I reported in one of my earlier stories. This kind of mission was his delight. We were to go from Italy to France "on the deck" and would therefore be undetected. This gave Spit the license to do his thing.

I was flying White four last man in the second flight. As I remember, the flying time from the coast of Italy to the coast of France was about two hours. Two hours at zero altitude and in formation is a long damned time, especially if your leader is concerned about the aircraft that are following him. But Spit didn't give a damn. If he could fly at three feet off the water, so could you. If he could make little wakes in the water with his props, so could you. What he didn't figure or care about is the fact that the trailing aircraft generally flew slightly below their flight leader. With Spit there was no "below."

I stayed a little above my flight and section leader, maybe three feet, and was working my tail off just to stay dry. Everything else was going along as planned until we were within sight of the French coast. All of a sudden, large spouts of water began to pop up in front of us. The Jerries had seen us coming, and for lack of better flak, they decided to use the large caliber coastal guns for anti-aircraft purposes. I don't know how big those guns were, but when their shells hit the water they made one hellova splash. The first salvo took us completely by surprise. We didn't know what the hell was going on, but it didn't take a whole lot of brains to know that if a plane hit one of those "waterspouts" it could ruin the whole day. But by the time Spit decided that higher could be better, we were in the splashes. My interest in good formation flying immediately took second place to my instinct for survival. I dodged one shell splash by about ten feet and in the next second gained about a hundred feet of altitude. The whole formation went to hell in a handbasket as we all made the same decisions, scattering as we gained altitude. It was the only horizontal flak I ever saw and I had no desire to see any more.

We all got back together again and went on with the mission and made it back with no casualties. But the experience made for good hangar talk for several weeks and it furthered all pilots' cynicism for missions that were to be "undetected" during penetration. Somehow, Jerry always knew we were coming and had a welcoming committee ready, but none quite as unusual as that one.

13.) RED FACES END OUR RED CROSS PARTY

All of us were genuinely appreciative of the efforts of the gals in the Red Cross Club in Foggia. Without a hellova lot to work with, poor accommodations and no entertainment, they did great job of making a little feeling of "home" for the pilots and air crews of the 15th. We, the pilots of the 71st, decided we should do something to show our appreciation, and so we organized an evening party for them at our field.

We had a movie and somebody rounded up a phonograph and some records. We had some beer and local wine, plus the 100 octane gin we all drank and some Coca-Cola, too. I don't remember how many girls came, but I'd guess a dozen at most and the party got off to a swinging start.

Sanitary facilities at the field were somewhat primitive, of the "outhouse" variety, and the one we used was a four holer made of plywood and cardboard with two-by-four supports. It served us well and we made special efforts to clean it up before the girls showed.

Everything was going along fine until about 2200 (10 P.M. to you civilians), when a group of the girls disappeared. We didn't pay much attention until a couple of them came back into the club with looks of horror on their faces. They collared our C.O. and dragged him off into a corner where a whispered discussion took place. The C.O. started to laugh, then controlled himself and looked properly concerned and dismayed. In a couple of minutes, he went around the room and gathered up three or four of the more sober pilots and followed the girls out the door. The rest of us didn't pay much attention to these goings-on because we were partying.

About fifteen minutes later, two Red Cross girls came back into the club, rounded up all the rest of their group, and hurried out the door without so much as a "thank you" or a "goodbye." We heard their transportation start up and rushed to the door just in time to see the whole group take off down the road. The party was obviously over and we didn't know why.

The C.O. reappeared with the three guys he'd taken with him, all laughing 'till the tears ran down their faces. It seems that one of the girls, who might be called heavy-set, had gone up to the latrine, plopped herself down on the seat, and the seat had broken. Her butt was about halfway in the hole, the sides of the seat had pinched in, and she was stuck. She couldn't get up or out! There were two other girls in the line and they tried to pry her out, but her weight and the way the board had broken made it impossible. So there she sat, firmly embedded with her pants below her knees. That's when her pals came to get help.

I wasn't one of the three who came to her rescue, thank God, but their description of the action left little to the imagination. After pulling and tearing and prying up the seat boards, they got her out, promised never to tell (fat chance), and left her with her friends. Everyone of the girls was embarrassed to tears and wanted nothing more than to "get out of Dodge."

We all felt sorry for the "stuckee" in spite of our laughter. We agreed never to tell the story to any other outfit, and we never did. Our reception at the Red Cross Club was a little restrained for a while after that, but after a while they, too, began to see the humor.

We didn't have any more parties.

14.) Doc Martin Loses His Desire To See The War

Every squadron had in its table of organization a Doctor, formally known as the Flight Surgeon. He was there to take care of the health problems, not only of the pilots but of all the enlisted personnel. The Flight Surgeons of fighter squadrons didn't get much surgical work on fighter pilots since very few who got wounded made it back to base. Bombers often brought back wounded crewman, but the fighter pilot flew and died alone. It's understandable then that Flight Surgeons in fighter squadrons got awfully bored, with no serious work to do.

The 71st's Doc was a hellova nice guy by the name of Martin. I never knew what or where his pre-war practice was. Rumor had it he was an OB-GYN from somewhere in the midwest, which seems logical knowing the Army's propensity for illogical duty assignments. In any event, he was bored and somehow dreamed up the idea that he ought to see the war we fought. He figured his only chance was to talk somebody into taking him on a mission in the squadron piggy-back. A piggy-back was usually an older airplane on which major surgery had been done. The radio equipment, normally stored behind the pilot's seat, was removed, the armor plate behind the pilot's seat was shortened or removed, the guns in the nose were removed and replaced by the radios. That left room for a person to crawl in behind the pilot and sit in a semi-crouched position with his legs on each side of the pilot. It wasn't a bad position for a short hop but got pretty uncomfortable after an hour or so. Taking a piggy-back on a combat mission meant going with no guns, reduced pilot protection and in an older plane.

While a lot of fighter pilots were considered crazy, nobody was crazy enough to entertain that idea, let alone act on it. But Doc kept after us and one day came up with a new idea. That day was another standdown and a bunch of us were sitting around in our officer club, drinking our standard 100 octane gin and grapefruit juice. We'd all had a couple when Doc came in, full of enthusiasm about his new idea.

At that time in Italy, there was heavy fighting on the ground at Cassino and Monte Cassino. It was a large and bloody battle and lasted for quite a while. Cassino was only about fifteen minutes by P38 from our strip and Doc wanted to see the battle. He twisted arms and promoted this idea for a half an hour when, obviously under the influence, I said, "O.K. Doc, if the C.O. says we can go, I'll take you." He went out of the club on the dead run and was back in nothing flat.

"Wiseman says if you're nuts enough to take me we can go."

I'd opened my big mouth so I was stuck. I had one more belt at my drink and away we went. We got my chute and a backpack for him, cranked up the piggy-back, and took off. I climbed to about 8000 or 9000 feet and headed for Cassino. I circled the mountain in an anti-clockwise direction and gave him a bird's eye view of the battlefield. While he took in the ground activity, I was watching the sky. There had been no enemy aircraft in that area for some time, but I wasn't about to get caught napping.

We'd gone around about three times when Doc came on the intercom. "I can't see anything from up here. Let's go down lower!"

"No way," I answered.

"What's the matter?" he said. "I thought you were a fighter pilot. You scared?"

That pissed me off and that, plus a skin full of gin, overcame any common sense I had. I stuck our nose down, swung around behind Monte Cassino and laid piggy-back right on the deck down of what used to be the main drag of Cassino.

Somebody had been watching us up high, because when we came through town we met a hail of small arms fire. There were tracers all over hell and we could see some of the Jerries shooting at us. We were clocking about 300, and it didn't take more than thirty seconds to clear the town and the valley and I headed up and home. Doc yelled. "Hey, that was fun—let's do it again!"

I didn't even give that idea the courtesy of any answer. I was all through giving Doc a thrill. He finally shut up and I let down to land. That's when the real fun started.

When I shoved the gear lever down, nothing happened. No green lights. No gear drag. I began to sober up in a hurry. I went through all the emergency procedures with no success. I finally gave up and called the tower and asked for flyby so they could look and tell me what, if anything, could be seen. When I went by the tower, they told me my nose gear was out about two feet but no main gear was visible. That left me and Doc with some decisions to make.

I climbed back up a couple of thousand feet and spoke to the Doc. "Martin," I said. "We've got two alternatives. We can climb higher and try to bail out or I can belly this thing in. If we decide to jump I'm sure I can get out, but I'm not so sure you can. And there's no way you can go first. If we belly this thing in, there's always the chance of fire and a problem with your getting out. What do you want to do?"

He'd been silent throughout all the flying back and forth and understood the problem as well as the possible results. I've got to give him credit for courage. "You're the pilot, Stub. Whichever way you think best."

I'd already made up my mind. We were going to put the airplane down. I called the tower, told them I was coming in, and started my approach. I'd never seen so many ambulances trucks, jeeps and spectators on the field in all my missions. I had the sneaking suspicion they were mostly for my passenger. Pilots were expendable - Flight Surgeons were not.

The actual landing was an anti-climax. When we touched down the nose wheel, it acted like a caster. We slid in on the steel matting, making a hellova racket, and wound up in a cloud of dust. I had the window down and I popped the canopy before we stopped sliding and got out fast. But not fast enough for the Doc. I don't know how he got out so fast, but he had his hand in the middle of my back, shoving all the way.

After all the great to-do settled down, Doc Martin and I wound up in his quarters. He had real bourbon whiskey, which helped settle our nerves and made the accident almost worth while.

We never did find out why the gear wouldn't come down. The bottom of the airplane was too torn up to see much, and I really didn't care, and the good doctor never suggested going up to see the war again.

15.) A LESSON LEARNED FROM A GREAT INSTRUCTOR SAVES MY LIFE

Larry Chapman was my instructor at War Eagle Field, where I went through Basic Flight training. Just getting the assignment to War Eagle was a tremendous advantage over being sent to a regular Army Air Force school. War Eagle Field was civilian operated and started out training pilots for the R.A.F. and Eagle Squadron. The instructors were pilots with years of experience, in contrast to the Air Force 2nd Lts. at the Army fields. Chappie, as he was known familiarly, was a good example. He had been, among other things, a crop duster, a barnstormer in Central America with a Fokker trimotor, and he had flown for both sides in the Spanish Civil War. I have no idea how many hours he had, but he had a lot.

Hatch, the "hot pilot," in a B13 at War Eagle Field, 1943.

I'll never forget my first sight of him. Along with the new class, I was sent to the ready rooms down on the flight line. We were lined up against a wall where we looked at all the instructors lined up on the opposite wall. I spotted this big, and I mean big and mean looking, bastard with a hook nose and a prominent beer belly. I nudged Earl Maple, my buddy standing next to me, and whispered, "I'll bet I draw that tough looking character." Sure enough, I did.

Chappie was, as I said, a big man. Well, over six feet and one of the few who looked tall in the back seat of a BT13, which was what we flew. Instead of the deep bass voice you'd expect from a man his size, he had a high, squeaky, gravely voice that could drive you up the wall over the intercom. But he could fly and he could teach his students to fly as well. Once he decided you could become a fighter pilot, he was a privilege to fly with.

One of his favorite extra-curricular activities was to fly over to Palmdale, where there were a bunch of P38s, and tease them into a dogfight. The 38 was a good 150 miles an hour faster than our BT, but we could turn inside of them at any speed. On several occasions, he showed me a move that drove the 38 pilots nuts. He'd let the 38 get into position at our 6 o'clock, crank down a little flaps, and then, when the 38 pilot came screaming in, he'd chop the power, kick hard right rudder and full left aileron. We'd skid almost straight up to the right and damned near come to a stop. The 38 would go streaking past on our left and below, Chappie would roll out, put on the power and look right up the 38's ass. Then he'd laugh like hell and go rat-tat-a-tat over the radio. It was great fun and we students got a big kick out of it.

On the 16th of June, 1994, the 71st was sent to escort some heavies to Vienna. Just below Lake Balaton, we got jumped but good. The whole squadron must have had its head up and locked, because a bunch of 109s hit us before we even had a chance to call a break. The first I knew, there a 109 was on my tail and pieces started flying off my airplane. I started a left turn, hit the belly tank button, and yanked down combat flaps. I could see the 109 in my rear view mirror and he was still turning inside of me. Without any conscious thought, I did the Chappie routine, chopped the power, hit hard right rudder and full left aileron, and went skidding off to the right and up. The 109's fire practically painted my maneuver as his hits went sliding away from my pilot's nacelle, across my left engine and out along my left wing. Then he went sailing past me with Gerry Osgood on his tail. I was, for the moment, out of trouble.

I tried to roll out and get a shot at the 109, but I'd rolled too far over and went into a spin. My left engine started smoking and I decided I'd better see about getting straight and level, feathering that smoky engine and start heading for home. It took me a hellova while and a lot of altitude before I got everything under control. I won't go into the details of getting back to base, but it took a long time. There wasn't anybody else around, and I had to get back some altitude so I began hedge-hopping back to Italy. The airplane would fly as long as I kept my airspeed up, but, with a large chunk of my left aileron, half my rudder and vertical stabilizer gone, and the engine out on that side, I couldn't maintain level flight when I slowed down. It became apparent that was going to be a serious problem when it came to landing. Too slow and I'd roll in, too fast and I'd run out of runway.

But the gear came down O.K. and I touched down on about the first six feet of our strip, burned up the brakes and stopped in time. I was towed to my hard stand and greeted as a long lost soul. I was the last one to get home. I also had a crew chief that was mad as hell at me for getting his airplane all shot up. Sadly, we'd lost three pilots that day.

I found out the next day the full extent of the damage to my ship. That 109 had shot off that part of my rudder and vertical stabilizer below the boom, had put a cannon shell into the coolant radiator on the inside of the left boom and had blown it clear off, had put a bunch of holes in my left main gas tank and shot up the oil lines in my left engine and had put enough cannon shells in the left aileron to cut it down to about three feet.

Without that instinctive application of Chappie's maneuver, I'd have been a dead duck.

After I got home in 1944, I learned that Chappie was gone. When War Eagle Field, our basic training station was closed, he went into the Military Air Transport flying cargo. His airplane disappeared somewhere over Central Africa on a trip from Florida to Cairo. It has never been found. Whatever happened, all of his skill could not save his life. He was a fine man and one hell of a pilot.

Damage from the June 16 mission. Cannon holes in the left aileron and wing.

Lawrence G. Chapman, flight instructor at War Eagle Field, who taught "Stub" the trick that saved his life.

16.) A B24 Crew Learns What "Break!" Means To A Fighter Pilot

Back in 1939, my father and I had been the Chevrolet dealers in Stockton, Cal. That winter I went to Detroit to attend a school for Chevrolet dealers' sons put on by Chevrolet Motor Division. It was a tough six week grind in the fundamentals of dealership management. There were twenty-odd young men attending and I drew a roommate by the name of Dick Kinman from Grand Island, Nebraska. We hit it off really well and became good friends. After graduation he went back to Grand Island and I went to Stockton. We corresponded a bit, but gradually the contacts came to an end and I, more or less, forgot Kinman.

As part of the foofaraw about the Ploesti mission, the July 8th issue of the Stars and Stripes newspaper carried a picture of me under the caption, "Agent of Sudden Death." (It took me a month to live that down. My squadron mates rode me unmercifully.) About a week after the photo appeared, the Air Force had a standdown and I was spending the afternoon flaked out in my tent when who should come busting in but Kinman! He had become a navigator in a 24 outfit down near Cerignola, and when he saw the picture he got his intelligence officer to find out what outfit I was in and where I was. He came up in a jeep and found me, and we had a great time for an hour getting up to date.

He was dying for a ride in a 38, so we made a deal, I'd take him piggyback riding if he'd get his pilot to give me a ride in their 24. Nothing much was doing that afternoon, so I got an O.K. from our C.O. to use the piggyback, and away I went. I gave Kinman the better part of an hour in the 38 and really wrung it out. I think I had more fun than he did, but he was thoroughly satisfied and we had a ball.

It wasn't too many days later that we stood down again, and I took my plane, the "Mon Amy," to the 24 field which was all of about a five minute flight. I buzzed the field but good before landing and got everybody's attention.

Hatch poses for Stars and Stripes after the Ploesti air battle.

I parked my ship and found Kinman waiting. We went up to operations where I met his pilot and we headed out to their plane on the flight line, met their flight engineer who was to accompany us, and climbed aboard.

I have to give the pilot credit. He put that big bird through its paces and wound up trying to shear a herd of sheep he found in a big pasture. He missed the sheep but he worried the hell out of one fighter pilot!

Finally we got some altitude and he turned the controls over to me. I flew it around a little gingerly for a while, got a feel for the plane, and discovered why all B24 pilots had muscular left arms. It took a lot of muscle to haul that bird around. About then the flight engineer, who was standing in the top turret, came on the intercom to tell us there was a 51 at about 5 o'clock high who looked like he was about to make a pass at us.

"Five o'clock," I asked?

"Yep - five o'clock," he answered.

"O.K.," I said, "when he starts his pass, let me know quick." In about five seconds the engineer came back, "He's starting it - high side pass!"

"Give me full power!" I yelled to the pilot in the left hand seat.

He rammed the throttles and props full forward and I, using both arms, racked that 24 around like a 38 answering a "Break right!" call. We came right and up so hard that the engineer fell out of the turret and Kinman fell out of his navigator's seat. We wound up head-on with that astonished 51 pilot and he broke it off fast. He'd never seen a 24 act like that before and I'll bet he never did again.

I got our 24 straight and level again, got the crew back in their seats, all laughing our heads off.

"Now you know how a fighter pilot reacts," I grinned. "Ain't it fun?"

I never saw Dick again. He survived the war, went back to Grand Island and took over the dealership. We sent Xmas cards back and forth for many years until he died of cancer at an early age. He always commented on his cards about our swap of rides. He was a good friend and a fine man.

17.) June 10, 1944 - A Bad Day At Ploesti

Almost any veteran who spent time in combat, whether on the ground, at sea or in the air, will tell you that there was one week or day or even an hour that will be forever engraved in his memory. He will recall it again and again, and while he may never speak of it to anyone else, it will stay fresh in his memory down through the years.

That time for me is June 10th, 1944, and the mission was over Ploesti, Romania. The 15th Air Force was based in Italy and was charged with carrying the air offensive to the Germans in the Balkans, Austria and southern Germany. Of all the targets the 15th attacked, the oil complex at Ploesti was one of, if not the, most important. The Ploesti oilfields supplied Germany with virtually all its crude oil and refined petroleum products. It was of supreme importance to the Axis and it was defended as strongly as possible. The 15th started its campaign of destruction on April 5, 1944, and continued until August 19th. During that time there were 5,479 heavy aircraft sorties which resulted in 223 lost bombers, a ratio of 4.1%. I do not have the totals for fighter losses during those months but they too were considerable. My Group went to Ploesti sixteen times over that period.

There was one part of the facility that the heavies seemingly could not hit. It was The Romano-Americano Oil Company's cracking towers that produced gasoline. In an effort to finish the job, some bright desk-bound planner conceived the idea of sending in some P38s to dive-bomb the target. In my opinion, and that of every one involved, it was a hair-brained scheme and in no way reflected reality. The bombers went in at 23,000 to 25,000 feet and took major losses from the flak. The 38s were to go in at 8,000 feet and dive into the flak.

We were briefed very early that morning. We were routed out at 0400, had some breakfast and went down to Group Headquarters for the briefing. When we walked in and sat down, it was apparent something unusual was in the air because the Group Commander, the Group Intelligence Officer

Flak over Ploesti. The "heavies" took the brunt of it, but fighter pilots sometimes got their share.

and all the other brass in the Group were in the room. When they went to the map and drew the line to Ploesti all of us kinda went "Uh Oh." And then, when they told us what the mission was, there was absolute silence in the briefing area - and utter disbelief. We are going 600 miles and surprise the Germans and dive bomb the Refinery? Somebody was insane. The briefing went on and we were informed that the 82nd Group would be the dive bombers and that we were selected to be the fighter cover for them. I cannot describe the sense of relief that went through that gathering of fighter pilots when we found out we weren't going to be the ones carrying a 1000 lb. bomb under one wing and a belly tank under the other, and that we wouldn't be the ones to dive into that unbelievable flak. The briefing went on, giving courses to fly, rendezvous points and weather information. We were a subdued group when we walked out and headed for our planes.

This was to be my 27th mission, and for the first time I was boosted up to the post of element leader or Green Three in the fourth flight. Our call sign was Cragmore, and I was flying (Mon Amy) my own plane, a P38-J15.

We were lucky. The weather was CAVU all the way there and back. Take-off at 0505 was normal and each squadron launched sixteen ships and three spares who would fill in if someone had to abort. We rendezvoused with the 82nd on schedule. Our orders were to go all the way on the deck, meaning as low as possible. As soon as we hopped over the Yugoslavian mountains, the Group Leader dropped us down to about 100 or 150 feet and away we went. In spite of the difficulty in keeping formation at that low level, we hit our IP right on time and started our programmed turn to the north toward Ploesti. However, the 82nd did not turn and we were forced to turn East again which tangled the two groups up and forced our Blue Flight out of our formation and into the 82nd. Then the 82nd decided to make the turn and we had to bail out westward to keep from colliding with them.

At that point we dropped our belly tanks and started to climb to the altitude we were supposed to reach to cover the 82nd. As we completed our turn, we flew right over an enemy airfield and in the pattern were four or five Dornier 217 transports. No fighter pilot could turn down a target like that and our Squadron leader, Johnny Shepherd, went after them. I followed my flight leader in the attack and wasted a few rounds of ammunition I needed badly a little later.

In all this turning and changing direction, I had fallen back of my Green one and two by about fifty or sixty yards. That little mistake saved my neck.

At this point we were no more than maybe 250 to 300 feet off the ground and we began to pull up sharply when somebody hollered "Cragmore - break left!" I instinctively looked to my left and there was a whole flock of FW190s headed in from 10 o'clock. We all broke hard to our left to meet them head on and, as I turned, a lone 190 came across in front of me. He was so close all I could see in my sight was the belly of his fuselage and the wing roots. He wasn't more than fifty or seventy-five yards away. I opened fire with my four 5 caliber and the 20mm cannon and damned near blew him in half with a two foot hole beneath his cockpit. Shooting at him pulled me further around to my right and I looked up at 2 o'clock and there were another four 190s.

I did the only thing I could do and pulled up into them and opened fire. The leader was about 150 to 200 yards away, nearly head on but slightly to my left. I set him on fire with a burst that went through the engine to the cockpit and wingroots. He rolled to his right and passed me on my left. I didn't see him crash but my gun camera showed the fire, and my wingman, Joe Morrison confirmed the crash. The other three went right over my head and down on the tail of Green one and two and shot both of them down.

I kept turning to my right, Morrison staying with me, and saw another 190 right up behind one of my tent mates, Joe Jackson, who was White four. I closed in on the 190 and tried to hit his cockpit but it was too late to save Joe. He rolled over and went in and was killed. I got the 190 and he followed Joe right into the ground.

I kept turning right, going quite slowly by then, with combat flaps down and burning off airspeed in the turns. I turned maybe another 50 degrees and saw one of our 38s coming head on at me with another 190 on his tail. I was still at no more than 250 or 300 feet and the 38 passed over me by about another fifty or seventy-five feet. I pulled my nose up and opened fire on the 190 who was also head on to me. I shot the bottom half of his engine off and he nosed down still shooting at me and I had to dump the wheel hard to get under him. He was burning when he went over me by about three feet and his right wing knocked about three inches off my left rudder.

Hatch's left rudder, with a cannon shell still in it, gives testimony to the Hatch luck.

As that 190 went over my head, I saw three more making at pass at me from my left. I broke into them so fast I lost Morrison, my wingman. I missed my shot that time and they went over me and down after Morrison. I saw two more of them diving at a 38 and I gave the lead one a burst and hit his left wing and shredded his aileron and he fell off to his left and went in. He was so low there was no chance to recover. I kept on going around to my left and shot at the second one. I knocked a bunch of pieces off his cowling and fuselage but I didn't have time to see what happened to him.

I looked up at two o'clock and saw another one coming right at me. It was too late for me to turn. I just shut my eyes and hunched down in my cockpit. I thought I'd bought the farm right then, but he missed me without even putting a hole in my ship. I think the reason he missed was that I was going so slowly that he overestimated my speed and over led me. I started to turn after him when he went in front of me and then I saw another plane closer and opened fire on him. I got about ten rounds off and my guns quit. I was out of ammunition. I got a few hits on him but didn't hurt him much.

I cannot overemphasize what a melee it was. There were our twelve 38s and somewhere between twenty-five and thirty 190s in a little hollow area with low hills on all sides. None of us were at more than 200 or 300 feet altitude and some were a lot lower. It was the wildest dog fight I was ever in before or after. There were aircraft going in, 38s and 190s, all over the place, It was a wild, wild few minutes. According to the mission report from our debriefing, the whole fight took place in less then six or eight minutes.

Suddenly I woke up to the fact that I was out of ammunition, 600 miles into enemy territory and all by my lonesome. I broke out of the area, jumped over the hills and went looking for some company. In only a few minutes, I found one of my squadron mates, Carl Hoenshell. I called him on the radio and we joined up. About then we heard my wingman, Morrison calling for help. He said he was on single engine and badly shot up and would someone please come and help him. Hoey and I turned back to look for

Joe. We finally picked him up at about 200 feet and got him headed in our direction. His airplane looked like a lace doily. The two 190s that had gone over me wound up on his tail. He was flying, but barely. I talked to Hoey and found out he was out of ammunition, too. We hadn't flown more than four or five minutes more when another 38 joined us. He was John Allen from the 94th squadron. We were happy to see him and hoped he had some ammo. When we called to ask, we found out his radio was out and we couldn't talk to him.

We hadn't gone more than twenty or thirty miles west and were just getting a little altitude when we ran into a bunch of flak. Morrison got separated again because he couldn't move as fast as we could and we had to go back again and find him.

We nursed Joe along for a long, long time and finally got out of Romania and into Yugoslavia and had climbed to about 12,000 feet. We had to ess back and forth over Joe because he couldn't maintain our airspeed on his one engine. As I was turning from one of these esses, I saw six 109s at about eight o'clock to us.

I hollered at Hoey, "Bogies? High at eight o'clock."

He saw them too and responded "Hold it — hold it. Morrison, hit the deck." Joe lost no time, stuck his nose down and headed for the deck.

Hoenshell, Allen and I held our turn and, when the 109s broke their formation and came at us from six o'clock, we turned up into them brave as hell, hoping we would scare them off by looking like we were ready for a fight. They didn't scare worth a damn. Hoey, acting as flight leader, waited a brief second and hollered, "Hit the deck!" I wasted no time doing just that, rolled over on my back and split-essed out of there.

One 109 took after me, and I got a glimpse of two after Hoey, but I don't know where the others went. There was an under cast beneath us, how thick we didn't know, and I didn't have the faintest idea whether there were mountains in the clouds or not, but there was no choice at that point. An ME 109 was chasing me and I had nothing left to fight with, so I went through that overcast so fast I didn't even see it! I was traveling close to 500 mph when I came out the bottom of the clouds screaming down a nice little valley between two high ridges. My guardian angel was still with me!

I kept going and, when I was sure I'd lost the 109, I pulled back up through the overcast and started looking for Hoey or Allen or Joe, but I couldn't see anyone. I heard Joe calling for help, but my fuel level was getting down to the point where I couldn't afford to go looking around anymore.

After a six-hour mission, Hatch poses, somewhat unwillingly, for another publicity photo, about a week after his historic June 10 mission.

When I landed back at our base, I was the first member of the squadron who had been in the fight to return. Blue flight had come in a short time before and had met no enemy. It was noon and my elapsed time on the mission was six hours, fifty-five minutes. I don't think I had enough gas left to make it around the circuit if I had missed my first approach. Next in were our Squadron Commander John Shepherd and my tent mate, O.E. Johnson. It turned out they had to land on the little island of Vis off the Yugo coast, which was held by a bunch of British commandos, and they had gotten enough fuel to get home.

Much later that evening, after debriefing, and a little "medicinal alcohol" that the flight surgeon put out, who should come wandering into our officers club but Joe Morrison. He'd gotten that wreck of an airplane across the Adriatic and dumped it in a pile on a field near Bari. To say that I was glad to see him is an understatement.

The two groups that had been elected to fly the mission were the 82nd and my Group, the 1st. Of the ninety-six aircraft that took off from Italy, eighty-five or six reached the target area. Of those, twenty-four were lost to enemy fighters or flak.

The 71st sent sixteen pilots out that day and lost eight of them. Of the eight lost, three were later found as prisoners of war, returned by the Russians after the war was over. Allen also became a prisoner and returned. Hoenshell is still listed as missing in action. Not a good day for the 71st.

After all the smoke and dust had settled, I was credited with five confirmed victories, one probable victory and one damaged. I'd have given them all back for one of ours.

18.) FORTY YEARS LATER, HISTORY IS REWRITTEN

There was a strange turn of events concerning the June 10th mission that didn't occur until 36 years afterwards. They brought to light a lot of information unknown until then and caused the rewriting of the 1st Fighter Group's history. Here's how it all came about.

There is a chap by the name of Carlos Marlow who has been, and is, the greatest collector of fighter pilots' autographs and pictures that I know of. His collection includes American, British, French, German, Italian, Russian and Japanese pilots - all Aces. Anyone who flew fighters and qualified as an Ace in his airforce was fair game for Carlos. At last count, he told me he was up to thirteen hundred names. He maintains a card file and every year each of us gets a birthday card. His devotion to his collection and his persistence is amazing.

Some time in early 1980, I got a letter from Carlos asking me if I would be interested in trying to develop a correspondence with one Edouard Neumann of Munich, Germany. In 1944 Neumann had been the commanding officer of the Luftwaffe Fighter Wing in their southeast sector. I jumped at the chance and wrote to the address I was given. Herr Neumann responded, and we carried on a slow, difficult correspondence for several years. I say "slow and difficult" because he didn't read or write English and I had no ability in German, so every letter had to be taken to someone and translated. It was from that correspondence that I learned of facts that stunned me.

Neumann's command included the Ploesti oilfields and he was aware of the combat on June 10th. He told me that, at that time, there were no German pilots and no German aircraft left in his area. He said that in the late spring all the regular Luftwaffe Squadrons were recalled to Germany to protect the homeland. The fighter defenses of Ploesti were manned by Rumanian pilots flying IAR-80s. The unit we tangled with was commanded by a man named Vizanty.

I dug around as best I could and found out the IAR-80 was Rumanian-built and was an excellent copy of the FW-190. Pictures of the two of them placed side by side showed some differences, but, in the air and in the heat of battle, telling them apart was close to impossible.

As an aside, I might add that, on that day, aircraft identification was the least of my concerns. The airplanes were shooting at me, they looked like 190s, and they acted like 190s. That was enough identification for me.

Armed with that amazing information, I went to the 1984 reunion of the lst Fighter Group Association and told my story. Not one pilot or intelligence officer had ever heard of the IAR-80 in 1944, let alone in 1984. It took some persuasion, but the Group Historian finally agreed that my information was correct, and he agreed to rewrite the history of the Group. Today all references to E.A. on June 10th name the IAS-80 as the enemy aircraft involved.

I've often wondered where the hell our intelligence was in 1944. Somebody must have known about that airplane!

19.) A Coward Gets His Comeuppance

There was a pilot in the 71st that nobody had any use for. He was a coward, pure and simple, and a gutless wonder. He'd had about a dozen aborts due to "mechanical reasons," each of them on a mission that promised to be tough. His crew chief hated him and the rest of the pilots ignored him. It was on June 10th, 1944, the day of the Ploesti mission, that he finally got his comeuppance.

I've written and many others have written about the mission, but I don't believe I've ever spoken about the debriefing meeting after I returned. I was the only one back who had been in the fight and everybody and his dog wanted to talk to me. I'd talked, described, and reflown the mission a dozen times when into the briefing room came O.E. and Johnny Shepherd, who had been the squadron leaders. They'd had to refuel on the island of Vis and were late returning. Included in the group in the room was the guy who had aborted that day, causing George Johnson, a spare, to fill in for him. George didn't make it back.

Before anybody could say a word, Shepherd walked over to the coward, reached out, yanked his wings off his shirt, and yelled. "You yellow bastard. You don't deserve to wear these wings. I watched a good man die today instead of you. Get out of my sight before I kill you!"

There was a stunned silence for several minutes. The coward ducked, turned, ran out of the room, and Shep threw his wings after him. After a while, the debriefing went on and as it broke up Wiseman, our C.O., came to me and said, "Stub, tomorrow morning go down and fly so and so's airplane and tell me if there's anything wrong with it."

I flew the plane the next day. And there wasn't anything wrong. I also got an earful from the crew chief who said there never had been anything wrong. We never saw that coward again. The brass ran his ass out of the squadron and he disappeared.

I've often wondered which took more courage - flying tough missions or staying around when you know your fellow pilots think you're a gutless coward.

20.) A DIFFERENT GROUP OF PILOTS IN ROME

D-Day in France and the fall of Rome in Italy happened almost simultaneously and our little Italian triumph got second billing. Still, it was a big deal for our theater. It didn't take long for the rear echelon types and the P.R. outfits to set up shop in Rome to get some publicity going. One of their bright ideas was to get the leading fighter aces of the 15th to Rome for a publicity show.

As the ranking 38 Ace, I was invited along with three 51 pilots - Sully Varnell, Sam Browne and Herky Green. I was somewhat overshadowed by those three. First of all, because they were Captains and Majors and I was a 2nd Lt., but even moreso because my five confirmed victories looked pretty small compared to their 15s, 16s, and 17s. There was also a B17 ball turret gunner with five confirmed, which diminished my effort even further. But we all had a good time, got our pictures taken and toured some of the sights. In the process, I had a most unusual experience.

One night after much conviviality at a hotel bar, I headed back up the Via Veneto to my hotel further up the hill. Rome was, of course, blacked out completely. There wasn't a light anywhere, and, while I was mobile, my steadiness of foot could have been better.

The Via Veneto has small trees planted between the sidewalk and the street. I suddenly heard a piano playing. It didn't take a music major to know immediately that the player was good. The sound seemed to be coming through a blacked out window of the building alongside of me and curiosity overcame my desire to go to bed. So I investigated.

I felt a wrought iron railing around what seemed to be a street level balcony, and the music got louder as I came closer. I climbed over the railing and groped around what I thought was a window only to feel heavy drapes. I pushed at the drapes and promptly tripped over the windowsill and fell flat on my face into the room beyond and into a blaze of light.

The music came to a sudden stop. I picked myself up off the floor and found myself in a room full of RAF types, blue uniforms, wings and shocked expressions.

I mumbled an apology of a sort and started to back out the window when one of the group broke out laughing in what was certainly not English. He led my by the hand over to the gathering. Another chap came up and spoke, in heavily accented English, saying something to the effect that as long as I was there I might as well join them in a drink. Another drink I didn't need, but under the circumstances it seemed best to accept.

It took a while before I finally understood they were Polish pilots in the RAF and had just been sent to Rome. In the course of conversation they found out I was an Ace and I was doomed. Everybody wanted to toast me and I, of course, had to drink each toast with them. I manfully strove to uphold the honor of the American Air Force and, while my memory isn't too good, I'm confident I must have accomplished that goal.

I woke up the next morning in my bed at my hotel without the faintest recollection of how I got there, and I had a God-awful hangover. Somebody must have carried me up the street and dumped me in bed. I doubt that I made it on my own.

The one real recollection I have of that party is that of the burning hatred those Polish pilots had for the Germans. Every one of them, it seemed, had lost family, friends and home during the German attack on Poland, and all they were living for was to kill Germans. Theirs was a personal war. Ours wasn't, for which we should all be thankful.

21.) MY C.O. GETS P.O.'D

Our Group Commander was Colonel Bob Richards, a West Point man and a damned fine officer. He was tough but fair, and he went by the book, West Point style. Among other things, we admired him for the way he handled the late summer influx of high ranking brass coming from the States to get some combat time on their records. We called them "juke box commandos," guys who had waited until the war had begun to wind down before they risked their necks. They came as Majors, Lt. Colonels, Colonels and even one Brigadier General. Other Groups catered to their rank and often gave them squadron and group lead assignments regardless of their lack of experience. Not Richards. When they flew in our group, they flew as any green pilot would, on the squadron leader's wing or as number two in other flights. In August, I flew one mission as group leader with a Colonel on my wing and a Brigadier General as White two. That was the kind of arrangement that tickled the hell out of us peasants.

In the first week of August I got a week of R and R on the Isle of Capri, the unofficial R and R center for the 15th Air Force. A squadron mate named Tony Noonan went with me, and we had a great time - seven whole days without a mission.

There must have been a couple of thousand Air Force officers and crews there and maybe a couple of hundred nurses and WAACs. Trying to get a little female companionship was, to say the least, difficult. The competition was fierce. But Tony and I made it. We met and latched onto two nurses from the Base Hospital in Naples. The one I squired around was from North Carolina, a nice gal in her mid-twenties, and, while she'd never made Miss Carolina in the Miss America contest, she was fun to be with. There was no hanky-panky. We just went swimming together, toured the Blue Grotto, and had a few meals together.

When we got ready to go back to work, I promised her I'd take her for piggy-back ride in 38 as soon as I could.

A week later, the squadron was on standdown for a couple of days, so I tried to reach her at the hospital. Making a personal call on Air Force telephone lines was almost impossible, but by lying a lot I managed to get through and made a date for the next day.

War isn't all hell. Hatch and Tony Noonan recover on the Isle of Capri on R and R. Their associate remains unidentified.

The following morning my troubles started. I went down to the line to get our piggy-back only to find it red lined. (Out of commission to you ground pounders.) I went down to the 94th to borrow theirs but it was also redlined. I tried the 27th and theirs had gone somewhere. I was in a sweat. My chances of getting another phone call through were slim and none, and I didn't want to stand her up. Then I remembered Colonel Bob had just gotten a brand new P38L and had it converted to a piggyback.

I raced up to Group Headquarters to find the Colonel and beg for his airplane. He wasn't there. I found Lt. Colonel Roney, the Group Exec., and asked his permission to borrow the airplane.

"I can't O.K. your taking the Colonel's airplane," he said, "You'll have to wait for him. He'll be back tomorrow."

"Colonel Roney," I said, "you aren't telling me I can't take the airplane, are you?"

"No," he answered, "I'm telling you I can't authorize you to."

With that, I headed for the line, got the crew chief to get the airplane ready and climbed aboard, fully expecting to make the trip and be back before the Colonel returned. It took less than fifteen minutes to cross Italy and land at Naples. I called my nurse, and we went for a ride. Everything was lovely. She enjoyed the trip. I enjoyed my hot pilot status and, after a quick hug, away I went for Foggia 3.

I made the usual 180 approach, threw the gear down in the turn, and suddenly all the fun went away. The gear wouldn't come down! No green lights and nothing in my little gear mirror. I started sweating. I called our tower and asked for a fly-by. They took a look as I passed the tower and told me the right gear door was open and nothing else. I pumped the manual gear actuator until I was worn out. I tried pulling some Gs in the hopes it would fall down. Nothing worked. About then I was having visions of court-martial, life in Leavenworth, everything up to a firing squad. But I had to land.

I put it down. It wasn't the best belly landing I ever made - that earlier one was better - and I climbed out with all the fire trucks and ambulances in attendance. I wasn't hurt, so they gave me a ride up to Group Headquarters.

When I went in, a Sergeant said, "The Colonel wants to see you - NOW!"

"He's back?," I asked. "Yes, sir, and not very happy!"

I went into the Colonel's office with all the enthusiasm of a man going to his execution, hit brace in front of his desk and said the mandatory words, "Lt. Hatch reporting as ordered, sir."

I won't go into the next fifteen or twenty minutes. Suffice it to say that he started three generations back, discussed my ancestry, my own idiocy and why I should be shot at sunrise. It was a masterful chewing out.

When he finished, he slammed a fist on the desk and said, "That's all, Lieutenant!" I fled. It could have been worse, I guess. His airplane was a mess but at least I wasn't going to be court-martialed.

I've often wondered if that little mishap had anything to do with the fact that I never made Captain.

22.) BOMBS DON'T ALWAYS DROP WHEN THEY'RE SUPPOSED TO

During the invasion of Southern France of August in 1944, the lst Fighter Group was sent to Corsica on what was called Temporary Duty, which meant pilots, ground crew and support personnel packed their belongings in a B4 bag and took off. We were lucky in that there was a French, or Corsican, building that we could camp out in near the airstrip, which meant we didn't have to sleep under the airplanes. All facilities were somewhat primitive but, all in all, it could have been worse.

We were close to a Corsican village called Ghisonacci and not too far away there was a beautiful but cold mountain stream which afforded swimming and fishing. We bought wine in the village and caught fish in the stream, both of which improved our diet. On the way from the airstrip to our quarters, we found a French rifle stuck in the ground by its bayonet with a helmet on the butt and an I.D. tag affixed to the helmet. It brought the war a little closer.

Our missions for the time we were there were all ground support work. We'd load up with belly tank on one side and a 500 lb. bomb on the other, take off and, when over the French coast, call in to Beachhead Control to get our target for that day. We had maps with the same coordinates that Control had, and the assignment would be at a certain set of coordinates. On the day that I found out bombs didn't always drop where intended, we were sent to bomb a small bridge north and west of our landfall.

Everything was S.O.P. until we had made our run and had dropped our bombs. Or so we thought. As we formed back up (there were only four of us in the flight) I checked the other ships and got a great shock. Number three in my flight had his bomb hanging down beneath his wing by the after-shackle. It hadn't come off. When you are the pilot, you cannot see your bomb beneath the center section of your wing, and this kid didn't know it was there. He probably should have felt the drag but he had said nothing.

I called him and said, "Red Three, your bomb is hung up."

He replied, "I didn't know that. What'll I do?"

"Try to get it off, dummy," I told him. "Use your manual release."

We normally dropped with the electric release button on the wheel, but had a backup manual release. I had the flight spread out a little just in case, and about then it dawned on me that, when the forward shackle released, it armed the bomb and anything it hit would cause a large explosion. I had him wait until we were out over water and then told him to try and get the damned thing off. The poor kid did everything but climb out and pull it off, but it wouldn't drop. Which left all of us in a quandary. I got him on the radio and told him he had two choices. He could either bail out and swim until Air-Sea Rescue showed up or he could go home and try to land. That last choice depended entirely on how far down the bomb hung and the extension of the airplanes gear. I had him lower his gear and I flew up under him to try to gauge how much clearance there was. It appeared the bomb was eight or ten inches short of the main gear in the down position, but what I didn't know was how much the gear's hydraulic shock absorber contracted upon landing.

He and I went back and forth over the possibilities several times until I told him again that it was his choice. Get out or chance the landing. He was evidently more scared of trying to bail out than getting blown up landing. He elected to take it home.

We headed back and I told our tower what the problem was and suggested they clear the runway and parking area. They seemed to think that made sense, so we flew around for a while. When the area cleared to land, I called the kid and said, "I'll take the flight in first. If you go first and don't make it, we won't have a runway to land on. Wait for clearance from the ground. O.K.?"   There was a kinda faint O.K. in return and we went on in, taxied to the far end of the runway and climbed out to watch.

I want to tell you I've seen a lot of landings by P38s, but I've never seen a grease job like that one. He could have landed on a field of eggs and not broken a one! He let it coast to a stop and made the fastest exit from a 38 cockpit I've ever seen. I went down in a jeep and picked him up. I know I was still shaking a bit and I'm damned sure he was. Doc Martin was helpful. He gave him a double shot of the medicinal whiskey and everybody went back to work. We had to fly another mission that afternoon, but I let the kid off the hook. I figured he'd had it for one day.

By the way, the armorers got the bomb off okay and it was armed. One of them told me later that there was about four and a half inches clearance between the nose fuse and the ground.

23.) LIFE WASN'T FAIR TO O.E.

I've mentioned O.E. Johnson a lot in these stories and for good reason. He was a hellova fine man and he was my closest friend from Williams Field to the end of my combat tour. He was the epitome of the phlegmatic Swede. He was always, or nearly always, calm, quiet and ready to listen. He was a damned good pilot - smooth, steady and a pleasure to fly formation with. But as a fighter pilot he had one drawback. He couldn't shoot. I don't think he could hit a barn if he was standing inside of it. I'm going to tell a story now that, had it been known at the time, would have resulted in both of us washing out of Cadet training at Williams.

One of our last hurdles in Advanced was qualifying in aerial gunnery. We were sent down to the gunnery range at Ajo, Arizona and checked out in AT-6s. The gunnery 6s were equipped with one .30 caliber machine gun mounted on the nose. We fired at a "sleeve" which was the target towed behind another 6. All our passes were high side passes, both right and left. Each student's gun was loaded with bullets, which were coated with a paint which, when fired through the sleeve, left a color mark. The object was to get as many holes in the sleeve as possible in your color without either running into the sleeve or shooting the tow plane down. Don't laugh. Both of those unwanted results occurred at one time or another.

Our class was down to the last run at the target when two things became apparent. One: I was in the lead for the gunnery trophy. Two: O.E. was about to flunk if he didn't shoot a very good score on the last day. If he flunked, he was probably through as a fighter pilot and maybe could be washed out.

The night before we flew the final runs, he and I talked in the barracks. Both of us were worried for him. Finally, I made a suggestion. Why not swap airplanes? I'd fly his target and he'd fly mine. If we got caught, we'd both be in real trouble. He flat refused at first, but I finally talked him into it and we agreed to make the switch.

Well, it worked and we got away with it. It took some fancy explaining as to how the scores changed so much, but we graduated and became Fighter Pilots. I scored high enough on the last run to qualify him, and he scored low enough to cost me the gunnery trophy. It was well worth it. He was a good buddy.

All of which brings us to the real unhappiness of O.E. He had flown most of the same missions I had, had been in the same fights, but after many missions could not claim even a damaged enemy aircraft. All of us were rooting for him to get at least one victory, and on one occasion we even tried to set something up for him. That came on a mission I didn't fly. I don't know the details of the incident, only the result.

It seems that in the course of the fight that day, O.E. maneuvered himself with some help from the other pilots, to a position right on the tail of a M.E. 109. He was dead astern at six o'clock within about 50 to 100 yards. He put the right sight dead on and pulled the trigger and took a beautiful picture! He had, in his excitement, flipped his arming switch to camera instead of guns! By the time he woke up to the problem, the 109 was long gone.

It took a while for him to live that one down, but I didn't have the heart to needle him.

There's one more story about O.E. that is truly funny, at least it was to me.

Late in the summer of 1944, there were only a handful of pilots in the squadron with any real combat experience, and by then the Jerries were more evident in their absence than in their presence. We'd go mission after mission with no enemy contact and then, all of a sudden, we'd run into a hellova fight. Those of us who were flying squadron lead were having a lot of trouble keeping the new boys, the recent replacement pilots, to maintain formation discipline, particularly on the return trip from a target. We raised hell time after time with little or no success.

One day prior to a mission on which O.E. was flying with me, I got together with him and proposed an idea.

"O.E.," I said, "when these guys start goofing off on the way home, I'm going to call a break just as if I'd seen bandits at 7 o'clock - no warnings - just 'break left'! Maybe they'll get the idea that the formation should stick together. That is, if they don't run into each other." He agreed and away we went.

It was the same old story. There was no enemy action, just a ride up and a ride back, a let-down off oxygen level for the smokers, and a formation

Lt. Hatch grins at the good advice offered on a flight-room sign.

that was loose as a goose. I bided my time until we were over the middle of Yugoslavia and then hit the mike.

"Cragmore - break left now!!"

I racked my ship hard left and up, dropped my belly tanks like it was the real thing, and acted like all hell was about to break loose. That formation scattered like a covey of quail, and I had a field day chewing ass all the way home.

We landed and hopped in the jeep that came to pick us up and rode down to O.E.'s plane. He was standing by his plane with his back to us and when we pulled up he turned and glared at me. "You son-of-a-bitch!" he yelled. I wondered what he was so pissed about and started to answer him when I took a good look. His flight suite was wet from his crotch to his knees. It only took a minute to figure out his problem and I started to laugh.

It seems that at the moment I called the break he had just commenced relieving himself into the relief tube. He had to turn loose of everything to grab the wheel with predictable results. He was mad at me for a week. One of my biggest regrets in post war years has been my inability to find O.E. His steadiness was a great counter to my sometimes wild and excitable nature. He remains in my heart as a true friend, a fine man and pilot I was proud to fly with.

24.) A German Pilot Earns Our Respect

One day, coming back from a mission up in Austria, we spotted a Fiesler Storch putting along way down below us. A Fiesler Storch was a German aircraft comparable to our artillery spotter aircraft. Kinda like a J3-Cub, only larger.

Well, hell, we had to have a go at the poor bastard, so down we went, all sixteen of us P38s. He was low, and when he saw us, he got a lot lower. I think all sixteen of us took shots at that Jerry and I'm sure some hits were made. We chased him around those Yugoslavian mountains for fifteen minutes and never shot him down. At first we began to get mad, and did a lot of cussing, but as time went on, it became funny, and all of us were laughing at our lack of success. Well, that guy flying the Storch was one hellova pilot, and he made us miss time and again. He could turn inside of us at any speed, could slow down to a crawl and hide in a canyon, and speed up again faster than we could adjust.

Finally our Red Leader called us on the radio and said, "Break it off, Cragmore. That guy's too good a pilot to kill just for the fun of it. Let's let him go." We all agreed, formed up again, made one last pass in formation, waggled our wings at him, and went home.

That Jerry pilot could make that little airplane do more tricks than any stunt pilot I ever saw. I was glad he survived.

25.) THE MISADVENTURES OF SPIDER

One of the pilots in the squadron was a guy we called "Spider." The nickname came from his physical appearance. He was a tall, skinny guy who seemed to be all arms and legs and little or no body. He was an old hand when I joined the squadron, and on one of my early missions I was his wing man in White Flight.

The take-off and form up of the squadron was normal and we headed northeast. About twenty miles out, Spider's airplane went ape. He was all over the sky, turning, diving, climbing and looking totally out of control. I moved away just to keep from getting run into. As usual, we were under strict radio silence, so I couldn't ask him what was wrong. I climbed up a bit until I could see into his cockpit. To my astonishment, I saw him stabbing right and left with the knife from his escape kit at bulges of bright yellow that were threatening to fill up the cockpit and squeeze him flat. It took me a couple of seconds to realize what his problem was.

The C.O. bottle on his life raft had gone off and the life raft was inflating. There wasn't room enough in the cockpit both for him and that raft, and he was trying to poke holes in it to deflate it. In another couple of minutes he peeled off and headed back to base, and I spent the rest of the mission laughing.

There was another "Spider" snafu on the base. We had never had an air raid on our field and didn't expect one, but one night when most of us were in our little "officer's club," the air raid sirens went off and some eager beaver pulled the switch on the generators that ran our lights. All of us decided discretion would be the better part of valor, and we tore out of the club and headed for the slit trenches that were dug outside our tents. The fact that they had been used as a convenient place to urinate for many months didn't seem to be a factor under the circumstances.

Between the club and the tent area we had set up a volleyball court complete with net. The only guy who forgot about it was - "Spider." He ran into the net, tore it down, and then got himself all wrapped up in it in the pitch dark. You could hear him squalling and cussing all the way to Foggia.

The air raid was a phony but, thanks to Spider, it was truly memorable. We never let Spider forget it.

Our "Officer Club" at Foggia 3. The canvas roof had weights on it, in order to hold it down.

26.) AN EASY TRIP TO ENGLAND - A TOUGH TRIP HOME

In September of 1994, the 8th Air Force decided to go with 51s and 47s in their fighter wings, which created a whole bunch of surplus P38s. The 15th had been crying for replacement airplanes and weren't getting any. The Pacific Theater was getting first crack at 38 production. So the 8th, out of the goodness of its heart, offered the used 38s to the 15th. Like all poor relations, we took what we could get.

The 1st Fighter Group got the call to go to England and fly the 38s back to Italy. When the squadron got the word that some of us were going to England, our first thought was that this was a chance to get some decent booze. All we had was an occasional beer and a lot of what we called 100 octane gin from the Italians. I was among those from the 71st who was picked to go, and by the time we left, I had a money belt around my waist with 1,500 bucks (invasion currency, of course) in it gathered from my squadron mates.

I don't remember the dates of the trip but it was in mid September. One evening, all of us were loaded into several B17s and away we went for England. I climbed into the bomb bay of our 17 and lay down on the B4 bags stowed there and went to sleep, trusting the crew not to open the bomb bay doors.

We landed at Burtonwood airdrome early the next morning, only to find that our 38s were not ready and wouldn't be for a week or more. Standard SNAFU. Lt. Col. Pope was in command of the group (he was from the 27th) and, being a nice guy, he got us orders to fly in the U.K. on military aircraft. He told us we could take off and see England - just be back in a week. He was lucky. The group was back in ten days.

I had a very close friend from Stockton named Jack Johnson whom I knew was in England. He was an enlisted man and had written me that he was Chief Clerk, Signal Division, Supreme Headquarters, so I decided to try to find him. I got a ride to London and started to find Supreme Headquarters. It wasn't easy. Most people didn't know where it was and those who did weren't talking. I finally got a guy at a U.S.O. club to tell me it was at a place called Bushey Park, near Wimbledon, so I took off.

Once I got there it wasn't difficult to find the Signal Division. There were plain signs everywhere. I walked into the building and was looking around when suddenly I saw Jack coming down the hall. He didn't recognize me and walked right past me. I called out, "What's the matter, Johnson, don't you recognize an old friend?" He turned around and about had a fit. He was more upset at my being in a restricted area than he was surprised at seeing me. After a while, he calmed down and we had old home week for a while. He took me in and introduced me to his Colonel and a Captain who were the only other members of the office.

To make a long story short, his Colonel gave him a five day pass and we took off. We went to Wimbledon to the house where he lived, where I met the English widow who took in boarders, and then off we went to his favorite pub. We got thoroughly smashed that evening and I learned something on the way home. This was the time of the V1 - the buzz-bombs - Hitler's first rockets. They made a peculiar noise as they flew, and as long as you could hear the noise, there was no danger. But when the engine quit, it was time to look for cover because that meant it was coming down.

We were walking along a blacked-out street when I heard one of the things chugging along seemingly quite close. Suddenly the chugging stopped. The next thing I knew, I was standing alone on the street. Johnson had disappeared down a concrete cellar entrance without a word of warning to me. I stopped, looked around and BOOM - the damned thing went off about two blocks away. There was no damage near us, but I was one mad pilot and I let Johnson know it! His response was that he figured everybody knew the drill, and he figured that I'd hit the dirt too. We had a bit of conversation about how visitors from Italy should be treated in England.

We went up to London the following day and spent the rest of the week together. We had some problems with the enlisted man/officer situation and solved it by going to enlisted men's clubs. An enlisted man couldn't get into an officer's club, but they couldn't throw an officer out of an enlisted man's club. We had a great time touring the sights, met a couple of female Free French Army Lieutenants, and toured other sights with them. But that's another story. And one I'll have to "take the Fifth" on—some things are better left to the imagination.

I got back to Burtonwood on time, and in a couple of days the group was ready to take off for Italy. I turned onto the runway with my group of four and punched the radio button to call the tower for permission to take off and promptly dropped both my belly tanks on the runway! It seems the buttons in this cockpit weren't the same as the buttons in my own airplane. Very embarrassing!

So, there I was - an abort - and I sat and watched the rest of the group take off, wondering how in hell I was going to get home. In about an hour, I felt much better. Five others returned for one reason or another, including Col. Pope, and I had some company. That was just the start of our troubles. We couldn't get clearance for six of us to fly across France so we sat. Finally, they shuffled us off to a F5 field south of London and they got busy trying to get us cleared.

Throughout my time in London, I tried every place I could think of to buy whiskey and hadn't gotten one bottle. I still had all the money I'd started with, and I could look forward to some unhappy pilots in Italy if I didn't score before we left.

I found the F5 group's mess officer and pleaded my case. To my delight, he allowed as how he might be able to help me - for a price. I finally got five cases of scotch from that bandit at five pounds per bottle. It cost me 1,250 bucks for sixty bottles but I was in no position to bargain. Then came another problem. How were we going to put sixty bottles of booze plus our personal gear in six P38s?

It took some real ingenuity to get it all stored, but between the six of us we got them aboard, and when our clearance came we took off, with Pope leading three and me leading the other three.

We climbed up to about 10,000 and headed across France in pretty good weather, but about three hours out we encountered a front and Pope started to climb to stay out of the weather and off instruments. None of us knew how good or bad the instrumentation in these planes was and going on top seemed sensible until I suddenly thought about the corked bottles we were carrying. If we went high enough we could blow the corks out of every bottle.

I called Pope on the radio, "Red leader," I said, "we go any higher we're gonna blow all the whiskey out of the bottles."

There was a long silence and then he came back. "You're right, White leader, we can't afford to blow 1,250 bucks. Form up on me, engage your gyros, and we'll hold it at 12,000."

In about five minutes we were in the soup and we stayed in the soup for a long, long time, flying formation on Pope, hoping for the best. We didn't know where we were, what the winds aloft were, or how long we were going to be forced to stay on instruments. We knew there were Alps down there somewhere that were pretty damned high, but we didn't know where.

It began to be "washer-cutter" time after a while. Nobody said anything. We just kept on flying and then all of a sudden we broke out into dazzling sunshine. You could hear the sighs of relief without a radio. The only problem was that when we looked down all we could see was ocean and we still didn't know where the hell we were.

Pope made the only choice and we turned back north. We dropped down under the overcast and went looking for some landmark. In a very few minutes we picked out the coast of southern France, got a half-assed position fix, and turned southeast for Italy. We made it back to Foggia with no further problems and no enemy activity and landed after nearly six and a half hours in the air and without much fuel left. But the best news of all was that all but one batch of the whiskey was intact. One set of bottles had blown its corks, leaving a luggage compartment with a heady aroma. Some of the ground crew spent considerable time with their heads in the compartment-breathing deeply. I scarfed one bottle for my crew chief.

The 71st was still drinking good scotch a month later when I left to go home. All in all, it was worth all the trouble.

27.) A Bad Pilot Can Kill Some Good Pilots

In the effort to get a squadron airborne, formed up and off on the mission in the least amount of time and fuel usage, all P38 groups took off in four ship formations, one flight at a time. We would taxi the flight out on the runway, set up the formation and start on our takeoff procedure. In a P38, that procedure was to put all your weight on the brakes, then run your engines up to takeoff power at 54 inches of mercury and 3000 rpm. The flight leader would call for a check and you'd answer O.K. with your position number. Then you'd watch the flight leader's ailerons and, when he wiggled them, you'd let go. It sounds difficult but with a little practice it became SOP. The one absolute requisite for wing men was to stay up close on your flight or section leader, and the closer the better. If you drifted back, you'd get sucked into his propwash, lose control, and ten times out of ten you'd buy the farm right then.

New pilots, getting their first go at formation takeoffs, were only too often afraid to stay up close to the leader. Three times I witnessed the tragic results.

The first was a mission on which I was Red Leader and had a brand new kid flying my wing on his first mission. We all lined up as usual, made the check, and I let her go. No matter what position you're flying, those first few seconds of takeoff demand your complete concentration. I paid attention to my problems and had no idea what was happening behind me until I heard the tower say, "Oh shit! Crash wagons go!" I looked in my rear view mirror and saw flame and smoke on my right on the ground, and a quick look to my right told me my number two man hadn't made it.

That afternoon at debriefing, I got the same old answer. Number two had fallen back at the start of the takeoff run, got caught in my propwash, went out of control, and that was all she wrote.

I witnessed another instance of this kind one day when I was Airdrome Officer. (On every mission takeoff, a flying officer had to be on the ground at the tower. I never did know why.) The mistake and the result were the same, except that I had to go to the crash site and try to get the pilot out. It was pretty hot around that cockpit, and I burned my hand trying to unhook the seat belt and parachute harness. We got him out but he didn't make it either.

The saddest instance of this kind of inexcusable foul up took place one afternoon on Corsica. One of our pilots had completed his tour, got his going home orders and was happily headed back to Foggia. The Exec picked a new boy to go with him and bring the mail back. On takeoff the new boy got caught in the propwash, skidded to his left and chewed the booms off the other airplane, killing both of them. Fifty-plus missions that pilot had flown and he dies when some ass-hole can't fly his airplane!

What did Ernie Gann write? "Fate is the hunter."

28.) GETTING HOME WASN'T EASY

There's an old adage that says, "All good things come to an end." That's true of bad things too - if you survive - and my tour of combat duty came to an end on the 6th of October, 1944, when I flew my last mission.

I didn't knew it was my last mission when I flew it. It was just mission number 59. I don't remember where we went but it couldn't have been very far since my Form 5 shows only three hours and fifteen minutes of flying time. I do remember the weather was lousy, so maybe we had an early return.

By October there were just four of us left of the group that had arrived in March. There was O.E. Johnson, Mel Hill, Bill Armstrong and me. We had been flying alternate missions for some time, always as squadron or group lead because we were the only really experienced pilots in the squadron. O.E. and I had been buddies since cadet days and Mel and Bill kinda hung together. I wasn't real close to either of the other two.

That evening Major Wiseman, our C.O., called the four of us into his office and told us we all had enough time to be eligible to return to the States, but that he needed us for a little while longer.

"If each of you will fly four more missions, I'll get you your Captaincies and cut your orders to go home. I'd like to keep you, but there will be no condemnation if you decide to return now. What do you want?"

If there was ever tough decision, this was one. We all wanted the promotion but four more could well be one too many. O.E., Mel and Bill were all single men, a little younger than I was. I was married and had a three year old son I hadn't seen in almost a year. Their responses were immediate. "We'll take the promotion!" I just sat there. In all honesty, I had just about run out of nerve. I'd flown fifty-nine missions, a few more than they had. I'd had about ten aborts besides the fifty-nine, was the only one who had been badly shot up a couple of times, and I had begun to think my string was about played out.

"Home Sweet Home" at Foggia Three. When the wind collapsed this "building," Hatch decided it was time to go home.

I looked at Wiseman and said, "Major, I'd like to think about the deal. Can I have until morning to give you an answer?"

"Sure, Stub," he said, "I know your situation is different. See me tomorrow morning."

O.E. and I went back to our tent and began to turn in. Not much was said by either of us as I remember. This was the kind of decision that a man had to make by himself. I wasn't as worried about my courage being questioned by my peers as I was about my feeling of running out on them.

As I've said, the weather had been poor all day and was rapidly getting worse. It was raining, the wind was blowing and it was getting cold. I finally went to sleep, still undecided. About 0200 a loud crash woke me up and an even louder noise followed as our tent collapsed. O.E. and I fell out of bed, dressed in our usual nightwear of shorts and a tee shirt, and tried to assess the damage. He found a flashlight and the light showed one hellova mess. My side of the tent had caved in, the rack that held all my uniforms had blown out in the mud, and the wind was busily making the mess worse.

We spent most of the rest of the night trying to find my clothes and making what repairs to the tent that we could. By daylight my decision had been made! I was getting the hell out of Sunny Italy as fast as I could and the hell with any promotions.

In the morning I took my wet, muddy self to Wiseman and said, "Lee, cut my orders. I'm going home!" He really was sympathetic. He knew of my family and was kind enough to say he didn't blame me.

It took some time to get the necessary paperwork together, time I used to try and get some uniforms cleaned by the laundry in Foggia. The laundry consisted of an Italian family with a tub for washing and some gasoline for cleaning wool. You furnished the soap. They got stuff pretty clean, but you had to wait a while before you put on any woolens. They smelled to high heaven of gasoline and you were scared to light a match anywhere near them.

At long last, I and a squadron mate named Ralph De Sutter got our orders and left for Naples and the Repple-Depple. That's Army talk for a Replacement Depot. We sat around there for several days waiting for a ship and late one night we were taken to the port and put aboard a ship. De Sutter and I shared a cabin, which wasn't too bad. It even had a workable head. We sailed in the wee small hours of that morning and woke up at sea. We were aboard a small French transport - no name ever given - along with a full ship load of officers from every branch of the service. In addition, down in the forward hold, there was a large number of German P.W.s bound for prison camps in the States. But best of all, the cooks were French and the meals were like nothing we'd seen since leaving home. How good? Well, let me put it this way. When I left the squadron I was down to about a hundred and fifty-five pounds, thirty or more pounds less than my normal weight. By the time we reached New York, I'd gained sixteen pounds.

Until the last two or three days out of New York the trip across was uneventful. We picked up a convoy as we entered the Atlantic and had a couple of destroyer types escorting us, plus a small aircraft carrier. I think the Navy called them C.V.s. All the pilots aboard our ship agreed we wanted no part of trying to land on that postage stamp of a flight deck. We took more than ten days to reach New York and the last couple were memorable.

That fall, a first class hurricane swept up the eastern seaboard and caused tremendous damage. Our convoy slowed down out at sea in hopes that the storm would blow itself out before we got there, but we caught the tail end of it anyway. It was rough! The seas were actually breaking over the flight deck of the carrier and sometimes over the deck of our transport. Ninety-five percent of the passengers aboard were seasick, and the latrines were a sight you wouldn't want to see. I couldn't help wondering what it was like down in the forward hold where the P.W.s were. I'm lucky. I don't get motion sickness of any kind, and for three days I scarfed up all the food at mealtimes that the sick guys couldn't eat.

The highlight of the whole trip, and one of the highlights of my life, came on the night we made port in New York. The storm had passed, and we sailed peacefully around the tip of Long Island, when suddenly the city loomed up before us with what seemed like every light in town burning brightly. Off to the port side, the Statue of Liberty stood framed in flood-lights. Every man on the ship was on deck, and down on the open foredeck the P.W.s were standing. There wasn't a sound for long minutes and then a mighty yell went up. We were home, and there weren't too many dry eyes in the crowd.

I couldn't help wondering what the Germans thought at the sight of the brightly lit-up city. They hadn't seen a city lit up for six years.

We disembarked that night and were bused over to Fort Dix and put up in some B.O.Q.s. It seemed to take forever to get our orders and our tickets to go to our various homes, but it was probably only a couple of days. I finally got mine, went to New York, boarded a train, and set off for California.

Six days later, I was still on the train and we hadn't even made Denver. Hell, I'd driven across the country in less time than that and I figured I'd be over age in grade before we got to Oakland. Ours was just a passenger train, which was the lowest priority, and we sat on every siding the rail-roads owned letting troop trains and freights go by. I was past being antsy to get home. I was a tangle of nerves, so when we got to Denver early one morning, I quietly departed the train and went looking for the airport. Then it dawned on me that, being in uniform, I needed a priority for an airplane seat and some kind of orders sending me where I wanted to go. In despera-tion I went looking for the ATC office in Denver and began to dream up a story that would hopefully work. I found ATC and, with the old Hatch luck working again, found an officer who was a sympathetic soul and who, after listening to my tale of woe, took pity on me. He not only made up some orders for me and got me a priority but actually paid for the ticket! If I could remember his name I'd put him my will. I raced to the airport, called my wife to tell her of the change in arrival, climbed on a DC3 and headed west.

That's about the end of it. I landed at SFO that afternoon and my grand-mother, my mother, my wife and my son were waiting behind the fence. I'll never, ever forget my son breaking away from his mother and racing across the apron yelling, "Daddy, daddy, daddy!" I scooped him up, hugged him, and went to greet the rest of the family. I really was finally home.

29.) SHOW BUSINESS IS FUN - FOR A WHILE

Along towards the end of my required stay at the R&R facility at the Del Mar Club in Santa Monica, I got a phone call telling me to report to the PR people there at the club. I had no idea what was brewing. But that it didn't make any difference. I had to report anyway.

When I got to the PR office, I was told there was a War Bond selling show in town called the Air Force Shot From The Sky Show. It seems they were short a few heroes and, lacking anyone better, I was to report immediately to the Lt. Colonel who was running the show. I squalled like a mashed cat and did everything but refuse to obey a direct order. I wanted no part of being trotted out as the resident hero for any show, let alone to start traveling all over the US without my wife and son. It didn't make a bit of difference. I got the direct order, told Amy what had come up, and went looking for the show's office.

I found the house trailer that served as an office, walked in and reported to the L.C. His name, along with that of so many others, has long since been forgotten.

The L.C. looked up at me from the orders I'd brought and said, "Herbert B. Hatch, Jr. is your name? Hmmmm. Are you by any chance the son of H.B. Hatch of Chevrolet?"

Taken aback, I answered. "Yes, I am."

The Colonel leaned back in his chair and grinned at me. "I used to be the editor of the *Automotive News* and I knew your father well!"

I damned near fell over. The *Automotive News* was the paper for the automobile industry and was highly regarded by everyone in the industry. I didn't know what I was getting into but it was nice to know I had a friend in camp.

I told him that Dad had died in April of 1944 and we spent quite a while talking about my father and the car business in general. We finally got around to the show and what was going to be my part in it.

The "Shot From The Sky" name for the show was an accurate description of what it was - a collection of enemy material that had been shot down, recovered and refurbished to become a kind of museum for the public to look at. The real purpose was to sell War Bonds to the audiences they attracted. That all sounded fine, but I need to know where I came in.

I soon found out. It seemed that the *piece de resistance* of the show took place each evening on the stage they had built. On it was the major part of a B17 fuselage, artfully lighted, and below the front of the stage was the touring orchestra.

The "hero of the week" was introduced over the P.A. system, and, when the orchestra began the Air Force Song, he was to walk out, pinned in a floodlight, go to the little podium, and then tell the audience why they ought to buy War Bonds.

The whole idea scared the hell out of me, but before I gave any of the dozen reasons why I couldn't do that, the Colonel dismissed me and suggested I tour the grounds and be back at 1800 that evening. I went back to the Del Mar Club, got ahold of Amy, and spent the rest of the day trying to figure out how to get out of this mess.

Having found no alternative, I showed up at the show's office on time and found the place in a high degree of excitement, but the Colonel was nowhere in sight. I found the guy who acted as producer and managed to get him to hold still long enough to tell me that I was to be on at 2200 and was to wait in the wing of the stage for my cue, which was the Air Force Song.

"Where's my script?" I asked.

"Script?" he said, "There ain't no script. Just go out there and tell 'em you're an effing hero and you think they oughta buy bonds." And with that he disappeared.

I was in a state of shock, and was about to go into a complete state of paralysis. Then, standing in the wing waiting to go on, I looked down and saw a full squadron of brass go by, led by an officer with a circle of five stars on his shoulder. There was only one five star general in the Air Force and he was Gen. Hap Arnold, the Commander in Chief. As I said, near paralysis set in, but before I could totally collapse, the orchestra took off on the Air Force Song. The P.A. system blared out my name, rank, decoration and previous duty and I was on! I walked out into the floodlight, reached the podium before I fell down, and started to talk.

From that moment until today I haven't the faintest recollection of what I said or how long it took to say it. I finished, stepped back, saluted the brass in the front row, and walked off. I went back to the Club, got Amy and headed for the nearest bar, expecting a court martial the next morning.

The phone rang the next morning at some ungodly hour and the Colonel was on the other end. He was so excited he didn't make much sense, but the gist of his message was an order for me to get my butt over to the show at once. I went and found out why all the excitement. It seemed that General Arnold and the other brass were very impressed with the show, including my talk, and had only one complaint. The show wasn't big enough. To cure that problem, the show personnel were to get more material, including some flyable enemy airplanes and make plans to open in a month in the LA coliseum. That sounded great for the Colonel, but not of much interest to me, until he informed me that I was the one chosen to go back to Wright-Patterson Air Force Base where all the captured enemy material was kept. I was to find out what was available and get it shipped to California. He handed me a set of signed orders which included the words "by order of General H. Arnold, Commanding." I was on my way by air that afternoon, leaving Amy to get herself back to Oakland where she could stay with my mother.

To say my reception at Wright-Patterson was cool is an understatement. They weren't at all happy to have their toys taken away. I was escorted by a Colonel Council who made me very aware of the disparity in our ranks and who wasn't at all helpful in spite of my orders. But then, about the second day I was there, another unexpected event took place.

The Colonel and I were walking through the headquarters area of the air Force Materiel Command when I noticed a name sign and a picture of the Commanding Officer of the Materiel Command. The name was General Wm. F. Knudsen.

I stopped and said to Council, "Is the General in his office today?"

"I suppose so, Lieutenant, why?"

"If he is, I'd like very much to say hello," I answered. "I've known General Knudsen for many years." He wasn't much interested in that idea, so I took the bull by the horns, walked up to the WAAF officer who was sitting at a desk in front of the doors to the General's office, and made my pitch. She wasn't much interested either, but I insisted and finally got her to pick up the phone and tell the General that were was a Lt. H.B. Hatch, Jr. at her desk who wanted to see him. The expression on her face at this response was something to see.

She jumped up, took my arm and said, "The General wants to see you right now!" I thought Council would faint.

I walked to the massive doors of the office, opened them, walked across a half mile of red carpet, came to attention in front of the desk and started to execute a snappy salute. General Knudsen got up, walked around his desk, put his hand out and said, "Never mind the salute, Junior, we don't go for that stuff very much around here. Come sit down." We had a most pleasant conversation for about fifteen minutes, and when I told him why I was at Wright-Patterson, he turned to Colonel Council, who had been taking this all in, and said something to the effect that the Colonel should see to it I got what I wanted for the show.

I should probably digress for a moment here to explain my reception by General Knudsen. He was Bill Knudsen to every one in the General Motors Corporation. He had been one of the real movers and shakers in GM. He was the industry's number one production expert and he, along with Alfred P. Sloan, had brought GM to where it was before the war. My father had worked for Knudsen in Chevrolet and they had formed a close relationship. Bill Knudsen was a big enough man to transfer that relationship to Bert Hatch's son.

After that meeting, I had no trouble with Colonel Council or anyone else at the base and eventually sent a whole planeload of stuff to California. I also got an me-109, a JU88, and a Japanese Zero flown out for the show.

When I got back to Santa Monica, I still didn't want to stay with the show and go touring. I wanted an assignment where I could have the family together. I leaned hard on the L.C. (who loved my story about Gen. Knudsen) and he agreed to turn me loose. Two weeks later, I found out what a mistake I'd made when I got my orders to report to Kingman Army Air Base at Kingman, Arizona.

30.) A TOUGH SQUADRON TO COMMAND

Kingman Army Air Base was a training center for enlisted personnel who were slated to be gunners on 17s, 24s, and 29s. There were many different training facilities on the base. The final weeks of the program consisted of air to air gunnery practice with gun camera shooting at simulated attacks by P39s flown by thoroughly unhappy fighter pilots who hated Kingman, hated the duty, and didn't like the airplanes they flew.

The town of Kingman was small and dirty with most of the bars and restaurants off limits to Army personnel. There were no houses or apartments to rent for married officers. When Amy, Brooks and I arrived, we

Hatch in Boulder City, Nevada, with fellow instructors, Bill Armstrong and Arthur Hoodecheck.

found that the closest place we could rent was some ninety-five miles north in the town of Boulder City, Nevada. There was no way I could commute on an A gasoline card which gave me just four gallons a week. So I spent weekdays in the BOQ and managed to get home most weekends. Without a doubt, it was the worst posting I ever had.

I'd been at Kingman about four months when I got a call to report to Major Andersen, who had the overall command of the student gunner squadrons.

I reported as ordered and was informed that I had been chosen to take command of a new group that had arrived the day before. I wasn't very thrilled at the additional duty and tried to convince the Major that someone else could probably do a better job. I'll never forget his response.

"Lt. Hatch, this command requires an officer with combat experience. Your record in the 15th fits the requirements better than any other officer on the base, and you are the best one I have to handle this group." He paused and then dropped the bomb. "You see, all the enlisted men in this group are, like you, combat returnees who have flown at least one tour in Europe!"

I was stunned. "You mean these men are being sent back to basic gunnery school after flying a tour?"

"That's right, and, as I'm sure you can imagine, they aren't very happy," he answered. "It's going to take someone like you who can command their respect to handle the situation and you're it!"

There wasn't much I could do. Orders are orders and I had mine, so I set out for the barracks area where the group was. There was a standard GI barracks down at the end of barracks row and a small office next to it. I was dressed in sun-tans with no ribbons, just my wings.

When I opened the door of the office and walked in, there were three or four men sitting and standing there. Somebody had courtesy enough to call attention as I walked in. I gave them at ease and asked who was acting as squadron commander.

A big, tall red-headed man wearing Master Sergeants stripes stepped forward and said, "I am, sir."

"I'm relieving you, Sergeant," I said. "I'm Lt. Hatch and I've been assigned as squadron commander."

He looked at me with a sour grin. "I'm glad to see you, sir." he said. "What is your pleasure?"

I'd been thinking hard on the way down to the squadron and had made up my mind that I'd have to establish some rapport with these men in a hurry or I was going to be in deep trouble. So I said to the Sergeant, "Are all the men in the barracks area?"

"Yes sir," he answered. "O.K. Fall them out in front - no particular formation - I'd like to talk to them."

In about five or ten minutes, I was standing on a chair looking at 130 disgruntled men. There wasn't one of them wearing less than three stripes and there were many in higher grades. I looked them over for a minute or so and then spoke as I had planned.

"My name is Hatch and I'm a returned P38 pilot from the lst Fighter Group, 15th Air Force. I'm just as pissed off at being here as you are. I'm a fighter pilot with 59 missions behind me, not a training commando. But the Air Force, in its great wisdom, sent me here and gave me the job of running this outfit whether I wanted to or not. Having learned the hard way that the Air Force can't make you do anything, but it can damned well make you <u>wish</u> you had, I'm going to do my best to do a good job of it. You can be sure of one thing; I know and understand how you feel, and all I'm asking at this time is your cooperation in making the best of a lousy deal."

I waited a moment or two to try to get a feel of their response. I didn't get much. I went on.

"How many of you were in the 15th? Let me see your hands." I got something slightly less than half of the group. "The rest of you were 8th?" There were nods and a few hands raised. "You who are in the 15th, I'm sure you are familiar with the lst Fighter Group, and I'm just as sure I've escorted most of you on one mission or another. You and I are lucky. There's a whole lot of guys like us who didn't make it. As bad as you think this duty is, we're here and they aren't. That's some consolation." I paused again and finished by saying, "I'll do all I can to make your time here as easy as I can. I ask you do the same for me. Dismissed."

I went back into the office and made my first, and best, decision. I made the red-headed Master Sergeant my first sergeant and asked him what he thought the first order of business ought to be. His response was that something had to be done to afford the troops some place for recreation. The barracks were empty, just cots and foot lockers, and what was supposed to be the rec-room was just a big empty area.

"What do you think we should have?" I asked.

"Well," he answered, "we ought to have stuff like ping-pong tables, or

Hatch (left) with two of his comrades, following awarding of the Distinguished Flying Cross at Kingsman AFB, May 1945.

a pool table, some furniture, a radio and maybe a juke box." I listened, agreed and didn't have any idea where I could find such amenities.

We talked for a while, and as I stood up to go, he stopped me and said, "You made a pretty good start this morning, Lieutenant. Maybe we can make this work out." That was beautiful music to my ears.

I've forgotten just how I came to remember a man in L.A. whom I had met years before and who had been a friend of my parents in days gone by, but I remembered his name and the fact that he owned one of the largest funeral parlors in L.A. It was sheer desperation that made me take the long shot of calling him and telling him of my problem. His response was immediate. "Sure, I'll try to help. Why don't you come to L.A., meet with me and some of my friends, tell us what you need, and we'll see what we can do."

I got the O.K. to fly to L.A. in a 39, met with him and three other men, made my pitch and flew back. I was hopeful, but not optimistic.

Ten days later he called me. "I've already got a lot of the things you wanted. Can you get some trucks and come get them?" "Some trucks?" I asked. "How many will I need?"

"Depends on how big they are," he said, "but you'd better bring three or four."

I won't go into the details of how I got the trucks, 6-by-6s, some drivers and permission to go to LA. Suffice it to say they went. I remember the look on the face of the drivers when they got back. It was Christmas on the desert! We got a juke box with a huge pile of records, pool tables and balls, a ping-pong table with paddles and balls, a half a dozen easy chairs, a sofa, a coke machine with six cases of coke and, to top it off, fancy curtains for the windows. My position as squadron commander was set in stone!

I'm proud to say that, over the next few months of my command, my squadron of teed-off G.I.s was not only well behaved but, as the crowning glory, took the guidon as the best drilled squadron. This is not to say there weren't problems during those months. In any group of a hundred and thirty men, there will be recalcitrants and misfits. I had more than one occasion to apply the Articles of War punishments and we had one court-martial.

One Sunday, I was presented with the D.F.C., which had been awarded but not presented way back in Italy. The squadron of their own accord moved from the last position on the field to the first and, when they passed in review, gave me the "eyes right" salute. That was almost as good an award as my DFC.

They finished their classes about the same time I was transferred to Yucca, and I'm still proud of them and of my success with them.

31.) "THE PIN BALL MACHINE"

I've already indicated what I thought about Kingman Army Air Base, so I won't belabor that point. As time went on, Kingman didn't get any better.

The base existed to train aerial gunners for 17s and 24s, and the training was comprised basically of shooting gun camera film at attacking P39s. It became apparent after a while that the gun camera practice wasn't getting the job done. With a little practice, the trainees could take really good pictures, but when they got into the real war and started shooting real 50 caliber machine guns that jumped all over the place when they were fired instead of the nice quiet purr of a camera, they couldn't hit the broad side of a barn. So some bunch of smart, and I'm sure non-flying, types dreamed up the Frangible Bullet Program.

Simply put, they devised a plastic bullet that had characteristics close to a real bullet but one that would shatter when it hit a hard surface. Then they had to come up with that hard surface.

The Bell P63 was as good an airplane as its predecessor the 39 was bad. It was larger and had more power. It was a pleasure to fly. They picked it to become the "hard surface."

They made it the "hard surface" by the simple action of sheathing the airplane in armor plate, including the fuselage, wings, tail assembly, and even the cockpit, which was closed in with bullet proof glass. I have no idea how much weight was added in this process, but I do know there was no increase in engine power and no increase in the power output of the electric motors that drove the flaps and gear. The airplane became the living example of a "rock with some feathers on its tail." Kingman was picked as one of the first schools to inaugurate the program.

I was relieved of my training squadron command, and, along with the rest of the fighter pilots at Kingman, was sent down to Yucca, a field another fifty miles further out in the desert. We started flying this monstrosity in May. I do not recall any particular check out program. We just got in the plane, found out what we could do and what we could not do, trying to not kill anybody in the process.

I don't know if Yucca is in the Mojave or Sonoran desert and it doesn't matter. One is just as hot as the other, and Yucca was hot. High temperatures mean thin air and little lift. It took almost the whole runway to get one of those airplanes off the ground. Its rate of climb was ridiculous. It was logy and heavy on the controls in the air, but the real problems came in trying to land.

Like all Bell airplanes, everything on the airplane was electrically operated, including gear and flaps. The prop was O.K., but as I said, the motors operating the gear and flaps hadn't been beefed up to accommodate the extra weight. You couldn't get the gear down at more than 165 mph and the damned thing would stall cold at 150 to 155. And when it stalled, it just quit flying. We finally figured out a way to get the gear down with relative safety. We'd come into the down wind leg at about 160-165, flip the gear switch down, and then rack the airplane into as tight a 360 as we dared. The centrifugal force of the turn helped the gear down and speeded up the process. With gear and flaps down, we'd fly the downwind at 160-165, slow to 155 on base and finally come over the fence at 155 and fly in onto the ground. Also of interest was the fact that the brakes hadn't been increased in size either, and you could run out of runway in hurry. Fortunately, there was a nice soft, sandy overrun at the end of the paved area. It got used a lot.

But the crowning glory of this so-called airplane is how it earned its name. The entire armored surface of the ship was sensitized to record any hits made by the frangible bullets, and in the cockpit there was a "hit meter" that counted them. Hence "The Pinball Machine."

It was some kind of duty for recently returned combat pilots who had spent many months trying not to get hit!

32.) MY GUARDIAN ANGEL SAVES ME AGAIN

As I said in the story of Hoodecheck's return, the Del Mar Club in Santa Monica was the location of R&R for most of the returnees who lived in the western half of the United States. Wives were welcome and Amy and I had a very pleasant couple of weeks there.

During that time, we got acquainted with a Major from Denver who had been a P 47 pilot with either the 8th or 12th Air Force. He really took a shine to us and, despite the difference in rank, we enjoyed each other's company. He had been studying to be an opera singer before the war and had a tremendous voice.

The three of us were in my borrowed 1938 Cadillac Fleetwood "doing" the night club strip on Sunset Blvd. We hit Ciros, the Mocambo, and a few others before starting back to Santa Monica. We were sailing along on Wilshire Blvd., somewhat over the speed limit, with the Major stretched out across the rear seat singing "Figaro - Figaro - Figaro" at the top of his lungs when I suddenly saw red lights and heard a siren. I wasn't in great shape, and I figured I was looking at a drunk driving charge and maybe a night in jail.

I pulled over to the curb, the traffic officer came up to my window, and a strange sequence of events began to take place. His flashlight showed him immediately that we were Air Force officers, one pretty darned good singer who wouldn't shut up, and one somewhat woozy Lieutenant behind the wheel. We told him we were recently returned fighter pilots staying at the R&R center in Santa Monica and the following conversation took place.

He said to me, "Fighter pilots, huh?"

"Yes, sir," I responded.

"What did you fly?"

"The Major in the back seat flew P47s and I flew P38s," I answered.

He showed the flashlight directly in my face. "Where did you fly 38s?"

"In Italy."

"What was your outfit?"

"I was in the 71st fighter squadron, 1st fighter group."

He reached down, opened my door and asked me to get out. "You were in the 71st?"

"I sure was."

He looked hard at me. "Do you happen to remember a pilot by the name Ed Fisher?"

"Sure," I said, "He was assigned to my flight. I took him on his first two or three missions and, when I left, I think he got my airplane, named for this lady sitting next to me."

He took off his hat, ran his fingers through is hair, put it back on and said, "He's my son."

That ended our worries about a ticket. He made us follow him to an all night diner, filled us full of coffee, and pumped me for all the information I could remember about his boy. I told him the kid was a good pilot, which he really was, and told him how the war was winding down and a lot of the danger had passed. He wound up giving us bloody hell for drinking and driving, with a little tongue in cheek, and then shooed us out of the diner and sent us on our way.

God only knows what the odds were on finding that officer out of all the officers in the L.A. police department, on that beat, on that night. I guess the little angel that had been sitting on my cockpit for the past two years showed up just in time to bail me out again. Bless his little old halo.

33.) OVER AND OUT

Most of these stories represent a part of war that wasn't hell. Sherman was right when he said "War is hell" (Sherman was also credited with the saying that if he owned both hell and Texas, he'd live in hell and rent out Texas.), but if you have to fight one, a fighter pilot's war is by far the best way to fight. As a pilot of a single-seat airplane, thousands of feet above the mud, the mountains, and the forests, you rarely ever see the blood and misery that is so much a part of the poor damned ground pounder's war. You have no crew to worry about, or to bring home dead or wounded, as a bomber pilot does. For a fighter pilot, death, if it comes, is usually quick. A fighter pilot flies alone and dies alone and I, for one, would have it no other way.

A combat tour has a lasting effect on every man who survives one. And, for most of us who did, it has colored the rest of our lives. This book attempts to show that not all wartime experiencs are frightening or nerve-wracking. Humor exists and strange things amuse. I wouldn't take a million dollars for my World War II memories, but I wouldn't give a plugged nickel to do it again. Over and out.

Service Record

20 May 1942   Accepted for Aviation Cadet Training

29 Oct 1942   Ordered to Active Duty

09 Nov 1942   Started Preflight Training, Santa Ana, Cal
(injured, washed back 3 classes)

11 Mar 1943   Started Primary Flight School, Sequoias Field, Visalia, CA
(injured, sick, washed back 2 classes)

29 Jul 1943   Started Basic Flight Training, War Eagle Field,
Lancaster, CA

27 Sep 1943   Started Advanced Flight Training, Williams Field,
Chandler, AZ

05 Dec 1943   Graduated Pilot Training, 2nd Lt.

18 Dec 1943   Reported RTU Training, Salinas, CA

02 Jan 1944   Transferred to Santa Maria, CA

18 Mar 1944   Ordered to Hamilton Field, Cal for Overseas Processing

22 Mar 1944   Departed Hamilton Field

07 Apr 1944   Assigned 71st Fighter Squadron, 1st Fighter Group,
Salsola, Italy

16 Apr 1944   First Combat Mission

30 Apr 1944   First Enemy Contact

10 Jun 1944   Worst Combat Mission-Ploesti (five confirmed, one
probable, one damaged)

16 Jun 1944   Last Enemy contact (One Probable)

06 Oct 1944   Last Combat Mission

24 Oct 1944	Departed Italy to Return to USA
Nov-Jan 1945	Temporary Duty-Air Force "Shot from Sky Show"
15 Jan 1945	Assigned Kingman Army Air Base
15 Jun 1945	Assigned Will Rogers Field, OK
24 Jul 1945	Separated From Service, Camp Beale, Cal

Total Active Duty Time: 3 years, 2 months

CPSIA information can be obtained
at www.ICGtesting.com
Printed in the USA
JSHW020729170123
36336JS00001B/236